# PRAISE FOR *SEEKING DRAGONS*

"A must-have book for anyone who cares about dragon lore, mythology, or magick; or has a spiritual practice that encompasses these magnificent creatures. Whether you believe that dragons are symbols, archetypes, cryptids, or extinct species, this book will lead you into realms of the mind and spirit where few mortals tread…and you will be glad you made the journey."

—Amber K, Wiccan priestess and author

# SEEKING
# DRAGONS

© Virginia Chandler

## ABOUT THE AUTHOR

Virginia Chandler (Atlanta, GA) is the author of *Year of the Magickal Dragon* and *Seeking Dragons*. She has worked with John Matthews on several books focusing on Arthurian lore and legend, including *Arthurian Magic*. Virginia is also the author of several fiction books and a former first officer of the national organization Covenant of the Goddess. She is active in her local Druid and Pagan community, and she can be found online at VirginiaChandler.org.

CONNECTING *to* DRAGON ENERGY & MAGICK

# SEEKING
# DRAGONS

## VIRGINIA CHANDLER

LLEWELLYN PUBLICATIONS | WOODBURY, MINNESOTA

FIRST EDITION
First Printing, 2023

Based on book design by Samantha Peterson
Cover design by Shannon McKuhen
Cover illustration by Anne Stokes
Illustrations on pages 145, 148, 168–176 and 203 by Llewellyn Art Department
Interior chapter illustrations by Anne Stokes

Photography is used for illustrative purposes only. Persons depicted may not endorse
or represent the book's subject.

Llewellyn Publications is a registered trademark of Llewellyn Worldwide Ltd.

**Library of Congress Cataloging-in-Publication Data (Pending)**
ISBN: 978-0-7387-6970-7

Llewellyn Worldwide Ltd. does not participate in, endorse, or have any authority or responsibility concerning private business transactions between our authors and the public.

All mail addressed to the author is forwarded but the publisher cannot, unless specifically instructed by the author, give out an address or phone number.

Any internet references contained in this work are current at publication time, but the publisher cannot guarantee that a specific location will continue to be maintained. Please refer to the publisher's website for links to authors' websites and other sources.

Llewellyn Publications
A Division of Llewellyn Worldwide Ltd.
2143 Wooddale Drive
Woodbury, MN 55125-2989
www.llewellyn.com

Printed in the United States of America

## OTHER BOOKS BY VIRGINIA CHANDLER

*Arthurian Magic*

*The Northern Band*

*The Last Dragon of the North*

*Year of the Magickal Dragon*

These words are dedicated to the spirit of
the Ismenian Dragon
*From chaos, comes creation*
V. C. 2023

# ACKNOWLEDGMENTS

To my wife, Melody: you are everything.

To the team at Llewellyn, thank you for your amazing book "magick."

To Heather, thank you for believing in my writing and encouraging me.

To John M., thank you for the dragon words. Onward, always!

To Amy C., dragon sister, thank you for examining the text
with a scrutinizing eye.

To Debra S., Elder Mother, thank you for reading and approving this text.

To Kevin S., thank you for sharing your oil and incense secrets.

## DISCLAIMER

This book includes the use of and recipes for oil and incenses. Follow safety guidelines to dilute with a carrier oil when using as an anointing oil. A skin test is recommended prior to use of any oil. Place a small amount of the blended oil with carrier oil on the inside of your elbow, cover with a bandage, and check in 24 hours. If you experience any soreness, redness, or irritation, do not use the blend.

# CONTENTS

# SEEKING DRAGONS

W hat does it mean to "seek dragons"? How are dragons related to spiritual growth and transformation? How does seeking dragons relate to the old adage "sowing the dragon's teeth"? For that matter, what *is* "sowing the dragon's teeth"? Within this book, these questions are explored from an esoteric perspective. More to the point, this book is about dragon magick and working with dragon energy. It is intended as a guide for those who sense something mysterious and wise about dragons, and who want to work with that energy in a focused, magickal practice.

I have been working with dragon energy for over twenty-five years. It all started with a love for the dragon myths and folklore that I heard and read when I was quite young. The dragon that I first loved was Puff the Magic Dragon. I heard his song at a very young age, and it led me to many fantastical adventures. I loved to visualize a big, friendly dragon frolicking and playing along the seashore with a young child. Rather than "little Jackie," the child, of course, was me. I imagined that Puff was my powerful and faithful protector; no one was going to threaten me with a big dragon at my back!

Years later, as a young adult, I adopted a Neopagan spiritual path, and I made a new and wonderful discovery: not only could I touch and work with dragon energy in a magickal sense, but the dragons were very reciprocal to the energy partnership! What followed for me was (and still is) an esoteric path of energy work and spiritual growth inspired by and partnered with dragons. My personal dragon magick path is based on Scandinavian dragon lore and relies on a kinship with the energy of ice and snow. However, you will discover your own path with your own dragon companions as you practice dragon magick. As you establish your own dragon practice, seek to adapt your techniques and tools to your dragon allies and experiences.

## SOWING THE DRAGON'S TEETH

The original meaning of this phrase is to take action in an attempt to prevent problems, which in turn causes the problems. Esoterically, I think this phrase is deeper than that. Seeking dragons, working with their energy, and entwining their energy with your own is sowing the dragon's teeth. Simply put, by doing this type of energy work, you will be transformed, as will the energies with which you interact. There is dragon folklore included in this text that is designed to illustrate through story how others have experienced sowing the dragon's teeth.

Many of the deep secrets and much of the magick of the dragons can be discovered in the same folktales that have been told for centuries. These myths, folktales, songs, and poems hold the mysteries from and about dragons that have the potential to open the path to spiritual transformation and growth. As these mysteries are more often than not rather cleverly hidden,

I will demonstrate my methods for how to recognize the clues and find the key to unlocking them.

This first folklore selection is a familiar Greek tale from the ancient world, a tale of how a young man's encounter with dragon energy transforms him and his world.

## Folklore: Cadmus and the Dragon's Teeth

The tale of *Cadmus and the Founding of Thebes* includes a specific sowing the dragon's teeth episode. The Ismenian Dragon was a Greek dragon that guarded a sacred spring in ancient Greece. Like many of the Greek dragons, he was massive in size and mighty in strength. The Greek poet Ovid describes him as able to raise his head above the highest tree that grew near the spring of Ismene. He was the son of a god as well. A deadly and dangerous dragon, he also had venom, three rows of teeth, and a forked tongue.[1]

The destiny of the Ismenian Dragon is connected and, in fact, dependent on the actions and decision of Cadmus. Cadmus's tale is quite different from that of another Greek dragon hero, Jason of the Argonauts, who also sows the dragon's teeth. (We will explore Jason's tale in another chapter.) While Jason was tasked with a steady line of quests that were designed to either kill or elevate him, Cadmus is tasked by the Greek god Apollo with the founding of a city; he is appointed by the gods to be a king, the co-creator of a dynasty.

Cadmus's dragon tale begins as he is sent out into the world to find his missing sister, Europa, who had been abducted and hidden by Zeus. He can't go home without her, and once it becomes clear that he won't be able to find her, Cadmus visits the Oracle at Delphi to ask the priestess where he should live. The Oracle tells him that the god Apollo wants him to establish a new city of mighty warriors. The Oracle tells Cadmus that he will encounter a cow and he is to follow this cow until it stops. There, where the cow stands, Cadmus must build a city.

Cadmus does encounter a cow and follows the beast until it stops. Cadmus immediately begins to build an altar to Jove. He tasks a few of his traveling companions to fetch some water so they could prepare a proper sacrifice. The

---

1. Ovid, "Book 3," in *Metamorphoses* (New York: Penguin Classics, 2004), n.p.

companions dutifully set off and soon discover a nearby well. Unfortunately (for them), the well is fed by none other than the sacred spring of Ismene. And the spring of Ismene is dutifully guarded by the Ismenian Dragon, a son of Ares.

Cadmus's companions are quickly and effectively slain by the monstrous serpent dragon. When they do not return with the water, Cadmus goes in search of them to discover what has delayed them. Near the spring, he finds what remains of their broken bodies. Angry, Cadmus attacks the dragon with a savage fury. It is said that Cadmus used both sword and spear in his attack, but it was the blade that finally felled the son of Ares. Cadmus then took the water from the sacred spring and made his offering.

Ares was angered that his son, the Ismenian Dragon, had been killed, while Athena was apparently quite undisturbed by the dragon's death. In fact, she makes a personal appearance and advises Cadmus to do something else with the dragon: cut out the teeth and sow them on the nearby ground. Obediently, if still more than a bit bewildered, Cadmus ploughs the ground and the dragon's teeth are planted.

It does not take long for the sons of the dragon's teeth to emerge from the earth. Cadmus, much like his counterpart Jason, knows that he alone cannot defeat these mighty warriors. Athena aids Cadmus again by handing him a single stone. Athena tells him to throw it at one of the warriors and then wait.

Cadmus throws the stone and strikes one of the warriors on the head. The warrior is angered by the blow. Thinking that one of his brothers has attacked him, he lashes out. A bloody fight follows, and the brothers battle until the sun sets. When the day is done, as Cadmus looks on, only five of the warriors remain. Athena then advises Cadmus to approach and speak to the warriors. She urges Cadmus to invite them to join him in founding a new city, which he will name Thebes. Cadmus does as the goddess says despite being acutely aware that the warriors could slay him at any moment. Much to Cadmus's relief, the surviving warriors agree.

Thus, the mighty city of Thebes was founded by five sons of the dragon's teeth and the slayer of the Ismenian Dragon, Cadmus. The chaotic energy in this sowing of the dragon's teeth was managed to select the strongest of the warriors and let their strength be the foundation for a dynasty. Oddly, Ares seems to have forgiven Cadmus for killing his dragon son. The god offers his daughter, Harmonia, to be the new king's bride.[2]

Athena, meanwhile, does another curious thing: She had not given all of the dragon's teeth to Cadmus to sow; in fact, she had only given him half. The other half she gifted to the king of Colchis. There, the teeth of the Ismenian Dragon await the arrival of Jason.

The energy of the Ismenian Dragon did not stop with the dragon's death. Clearly, his teeth were a potent source of energetic potential. Cadmus carried the dragon's energy with him. Indeed, the residual energy from slaying the dragon seems to have given seed to guilt for taking the dragon's life.

As he grew older, Cadmus became weary of his life in Thebes. He felt no joy and was restless. He and Harmonia left Thebes and walked the Greek lands aimlessly. Yet, no matter how far they traveled, the old king could not escape the burden that weighed heavily upon him: He wondered if all those years ago, when he had slain the Ismenian Dragon, had he done wrong? Had Ares truly forgiven him?

When Cadmus finally voiced his regret and sorrow, he made a startling declaration: if killing the dragon had been wrong, then he wanted to spend the rest of his mortal life as a dragon. As soon as he spoke the words aloud, Cadmus and his wife became small serpents. The Ismenian Dragon's destiny had been fulfilled, while Cadmus and Harmonia were just beginning their journey as dragons.

## DRAGON ENERGY WORK

At the heart of this type of energy work is a practice of ritual and meditation that is solely focused on dragons. The wisdom, knowledge, and energy from the dragons can aid us in awakening our higher selves. Each chapter contains at least one meditation, exercises, and suggested journal responses. It is not a prerequisite for the reader to be a formally trained practitioner of any sort, as the book provides methods for creating sacred space, making an altar, and conducting a ritual.

---

2. Ovid, "Books 3 and 4," n.p.

Within these pages, you will discover deep meditations that are designed to connect you with these ancient energies. We will explore the path of transformation—for dragons and humans—and use the paths of those who have gone before us as a guide for our own journey.

The meditations, rituals, and other workings included in this text are relatively simple; in fact, it is intentional that any preparation is minimal, allowing the focus to be on the experiential aspects. The spells are included in appendix B, while the meditations are included at the end of each chapter.

## SOWING THE DRAGON'S TEETH IN A MAGICKAL PRACTICE

Working with dragon energy will be addressed in more detail in chapter 1. You will learn the preparation techniques for interacting with dragon energy, which include the esoteric concept of simple sacred space. Creating sacred space can be done with quiet, focused thoughts and gentle, relaxed breathing.

The meditations in this book follow a certain motif that you will come to recognize. In order to better focus on your experience, it is advised that you record the meditations included in this book or have someone that you trust read them to you.

## EXERCISES AND JOURNALING

Throughout this book you will also find esoteric exercises that coincide with each chapter's theme. The exercises are designed to enhance and empower dragon connections through simple interaction with energy. This is an experiential area of study, so to speak, and akin to a lab-type practice.

Recording your experiences as you engage with dragon energies can be a very rewarding and productive tool. After each meditation, there are suggested journal entries. If you already keep a journal, you can simply add these entries. If you are not a journal keeper, I strongly encourage you to do so and keep the journal close to you.

## DRAGON ARCHETYPES AND FOLKLORE

In my own seeking of dragons, I have discovered and now recognize dragon energy archetypes. Each archetype has a very specific energy, color, sound, and vibration. We will delve deeply into the archetypes and demonstrate how to work with each one in a respectful, safe, and productive manner.

What about serpents? Are the serpents from various myths and legends synonymous with dragons? This is a question that I have wondered in the past, and I still, on occasion, do ponder. However, for the purpose of this text, it is necessary to briefly explain my interpretation and my use of the word *serpent* in this book.

Serpents that are generally included in dragon legend, myth, and even historical text do seem to originate from a particular geographical area, namely the Mediterranean, Middle East, and Far East. Therefore, I see the Mediterranean *serpent* as being no different from the Anglo-Saxon *wyrm* or the Norse *ormr*. And, since it is true that the physical descriptions of the serpent, wyrm, and ormr (and other dragon types) differ so much, I simply see them all as different species of dragon kind. In short, *serpent*, as used in this book, does indeed refer to a particular *type* of dragon.

**CHAPTER ONE**

# DRAGONS
# OF THE PAST

Whether you "believe" in dragons or not, encountering an actual dragon in the modern physical world is not likely to happen. Seeking dragons, from an esoteric perspective, is a practice of reaching out to the spiritual realms where dragon energy and dragon spirits reside. Still, the idea of dragons being a part of the "real" world—our physical world—is exciting.

As a seeker of dragons, it is a worthwhile endeavor to investigate some of these alleged real-world dragon sightings. There is certainly potential that useful information for how (or how *not*) to find and interact with dragons could be discovered. Clues about ancient dragon worship as well as anatomical descriptions exist within these writings. Although most of these dragon sightings occurred in the distant past, several are based on observations that were written by respected scholars. These witnesses describe encounters with dragons from multiple geographical locations: India, Asia, Greece, and North America. Here are a few of those eyewitness accounts.

## HERODOTUS, 440 BCE

One of the oldest recorded dragon sightings comes from over two thousand years ago. In what the ancient world called "Arabia," the "Father of History," Herodotus, went seeking dragons. What he saw is nothing short of incredible:

> There is a place in Arabia, situated very near the city of Buto, to which I went, on hearing of some winged serpents; and when I arrived there, I saw bones and spines of serpents, in such quantities as it would be impossible to describe … The form of the serpent is like that of the water-snake; but he has wings without feathers, and as like as possible to the wings of a bat.[3]

Should we believe that Herodotus did indeed observe dragons? Consider that this curious traveler was more than just a casual tourist. The reason he was dubbed the "Father of History" by the first-century Roman statesman and writer Cicero was because Herodotus was the first known writer to use investigative methods as a crucial element for his historical writings. That being the case, when Herodotus writes of dragons and describes what he sees in such detail, it could be considered as scientific observation.

What Herodotus saw is that there were hundreds, perhaps even thousands, of winged dragons in Arabia in 440 BCE. Like the fate of other observed dragons, though, what happened to these creatures is unknown.

## ALEXANDER THE GREAT, 330 BCE

Alexander the Great, son of Philip II of Macedonia, is remembered as one of the greatest military generals of all time. Tutored by Aristotle as a youngster,

---

3. Herodotus, *The Histories of Herodotus*, trans. Henry Cary (New York: D. Appleton and Company, 1904), 111.

Alexander was an avid fan of reading, history, and medicine. He became king of Macedonia at the tender age of twenty after his father was assassinated. He died very young (age thirty-two) while he was still on a military campaign in the Middle East.

It was during Alexander's military campaign through the Middle East that he allegedly encountered a dragon in India. The description of this creature by Claudius Aelianus, a Roman author from the second century CE, provides impressive details: the dragon lives in a cave, is a massive 70 cubits, or 105 feet, in length, and has very keen vision and hearing. Alexander and his men did not see the dragon in full, but its head did emerge as the army passed the cave. The head alone apparently gave these warriors all a good fright as it stared at them and issued an ominous hiss. Aelianus recorded the incident as follows:

> Now as the army passed by the cavern and caused a noise, the Serpent was aware of it. (It has, you know, the sharpest hearing and the keenest sight of all animals.) And it hissed and snorted so violently that all were terrified and confounded. It was reported to measure 70 cubits although it was not visible in all its length, for it only put its head out. At any rate its eyes are said to have been the size of a large, round Macedonian shield.[4]

The locals considered the dragon to be sacred and worshipped it as a god. They implored Alexander not to slay it nor allow any of his men to do so. Whether he was respecting the Indian customs or acknowledging that he felt intimidated by the massive beast (or both), Alexander agreed, and the dragon was left in peace.

It is still a mystery as to why this dragon was considered sacred and how it was honored. Nevertheless, Alexander and Aelianus do provide a very clear reference to this dragon being viewed as a deity and worshipped as such.

---

4. Aelian, *On the Characteristics of Animals*, vol. 3, books 12–17, trans. A. F. Scholfield (London: William Heinemann, Ltd., 1959), 243, 245.

## ANGLO-SAXON CHRONICLE, 793 CE

King Alfred the Great's historical record, the *Anglo-Saxon Chronicle*, is a historical ledger that spans the years 1–1154 CE. Although, of course, Alfred's chronicle is dated using the Latin anno Domini, "in the year of our Lord." The chronicle begins in Anglo-Saxon or Old English, but the later entries are more Middle English. The actual scribes are unknown but were probably monks.

According to the entry for 793, the citizens of Northumbria had a rather dreadful and terrifying year. Dragons appeared in the sky, bringing with them angry storms. Soon after, a grim new age for England was heralded with the arrival of the Northmen in their longships at Lindisfarne Monastery. The Viking raids had begun and would continue for quite some time.

> A.D. 793. This year came dreadful fore-warnings over the land of the Northumbrians, terrifying the people most woefully: these were immense sheets of light rushing through the air, and whirlwinds, and fiery, dragons flying across the firmament. These tremendous tokens were soon followed by a great famine: and not long after, on the sixth day before the ides of January in the same year, the harrowing inroads of heathen men made lamentable havoc in the church of God in Holy-island, by rapine and slaughter. Siga died on the eighth day before the calends of March.[5]

Dragons are not mentioned anywhere else in the *Anglo-Saxon Chronicle*. It is possible, of course, that the dragons in this entry are simply the result of a rather frightened witness account of the events or the interpretation of the monk who recorded it. Did the people of Northumbria imagine the dragons as they cowered from the violent storms? Were the dragons simply the figureheads on the Northmen's longships? Or did fiery dragons, in fact, battle over the skies of Northumbria?

---

5. *The Anglo-Saxon Chronicle: Part 2: AD 750–919*, The Medieval & Classical Literature Library, accessed March 21, 2023, http://mcllibrary.org/Anglo/part2.html.

# MARCO POLO, THIRTEENTH CENTURY CE

Although he may not be remembered as a respected historian such as Herodotus or Claudius Aelianus, the written record of the travels of the thirteenth-century Venetian merchant Marco Polo nonetheless provide a very vivid account of the Far East, which at that time was a largely unknown and misunderstood part of the world. The politics, the travel routes, the culture—in fact, every facet of Polo's journey to the East—was and still is a focused glimpse through the eyes of a man who was amazed and astounded at what he experienced. The details that he recorded provide a very visceral experience, which made his book popular both then and now.

Polo, like Herodotus and Alexander the Great, saw many spectacular and wonderous things on his journeys. Among these observed wonders of the world were dragons. Interestingly, Polo makes a clear distinction between "snakes" and "serpents," which seems to be based on size and anatomical elements. The "serpents" had clawed feet, huge eyes, and sharp, huge teeth. Whatever it was that he saw, it frightened Marco Polo. What he recorded as a "dragon" was a creature that was able to devour men, tigers, and wolves whole.

> Here are found snakes and huge serpents, [crocodiles] ten paces in length, and ten spans in the girth of the body. ... The jaws are wide enough to swallow a man, the teeth are large and sharp, and their whole appearance is so formidable, that neither man, nor any kind of animal, can approach them without terror. ... After eating they drag themselves towards some lake, spring of water, or river, in order to drink. By their motion in this way along the shore, and their vast weight, they make a deep impression, as if a heavy beam had been drawn along the sands.[6]

What Polo describes here is often identified as a crocodile; if so, it would be a crocodile of very large size. The largest saltwater crocodiles documented from modern times are approximately twenty feet or so in length.

---

6. Marco Polo, *The Travels of Marco Polo,* trans. William Marsden, ed. Manuel Komroff (New York: Modern Library, 2001), 164–65.

Polo's serpent is slightly larger: around twenty-five feet long with a mouth big enough to swallow a human. While most alligators and crocodiles make nests and tend to stay out of sight, Polo's creatures lurk in caverns. While Polo does not use the word *dragon* in his journal entries, he does use the term *serpent*, which, as we have seen, is synonymous with dragon in many ancient cultures.

## WHERE HAVE ALL THE DRAGONS GONE?

Herodotus, Alexander the Great, Marco Polo, the *Anglo-Saxon Chronicle*, and more all record what they believed to be real dragon sightings. So, if there were dragons in the physical world dating from (at least) 440 BCE, what happened to them?

Natural death or death by predator are more than acceptable explanations to this question. Certainly, humans have hunted more than one species into or close to extinction. Or perhaps dragons have the power to remain unseen, either by some mysterious, deep magick or by extremely clever camouflage. In Asia, "other qualities of the dragon were that it could change its shape and size at will and disappear or reappear wherever it wished."[7] Any or all of these answers are possible. The conclusion, though, is the same: dragons in the physical world are rare if not impossible to find. So if we seek to connect with dragons now, then we would be best served to find another method. If it is pointless to physically search, how do you seek a dragon? We will address that question in the next chapter.

## DRAGONS OF THE PAST OVERVIEW

Dragons are not easy to find in any form, and even though there are records of physical dragons in our world, they have not been seen for hundreds, even thousands, of years. Despite the physical absence of dragons, we can still seek their wisdom because it is not physical dragons that we seek; it is their energy. By experiencing an energetic communion with the dragons, you are transformed.

---

7. Mark Cartwright, "The Dragon in Ancient China," World History Encyclopedia, September 29, 2017, https://www.worldhistory.org/article/1125/the-dragon-in-ancient-china/.

# CHAPTER TWO

---

# THE CALL OF
# THE DRAGON

Dragon energy is usually first experienced as a tingling of the senses that occurs whenever dragons are mentioned. It might be hearing a dragon story or seeing a visual image of a dragon. Whatever it is that sets off these sensations, the bursts of energy are potent and stimulating. What does it mean? Is this a valid energy connection to dragons?

That tingling sensation is indeed a very real connection with dragon energy. It is a feeling, a different type of emotion, that almost feels like a longing for something that was lost. This feeling is how raw dragon energy manifests in the physical world. A practice of dragon magick is, at its core, reaching out to the dragon spirits and establishing a relationship with them based on trust. Once you have done this, the dragon energy becomes a conduit for knowledge and wisdom as gifted by the dragons. This will be your reward. In turn, you will be a go-between, an ambassador of sorts, for dragons in the world of humans. So, what is the best way to answer the call of the dragon?

Answering the call of the dragon is a spiritual journey into and through the dragon realms. As stated before, to successfully traverse the gateways of dragon knowledge and wisdom, a trusting connection must be established with the dragons. This trust opens the way for meaningful energetic communion with dragon energy which, in turn, advances spiritual growth. This energy work will include meditation, ritual, and a deep delving into the dragon lore. If done with sincerity and without ego, a powerful link to the dragons will be created.

## BUILDING SACRED SPACE

As preparation for interacting with dragon energy, you should become familiar with the concept of sacred space. *Sacred space* is a physical area that has been spiritually cleansed and prepared for energetic communion between the physical world and the spiritual realms. The physical space may be a designated area of your home, outdoors in a special place, or both. The technique employed in this text can also be used to create a special area wherever you are by using quiet, focused thoughts and gentle, relaxed breathing.

The meditations and rituals included in this text are relatively simple; in fact, it is intentional that any preparation is minimal, thus allowing the focus to be on the experiential aspects of interacting with dragon energy. There is no "going through the motions" with dragon ritual; the seeking of communion with dragons will be an empty void of words and images if the seeker does not *feel the energy.*

### Preparing Sacred Space

To prepare sacred space, a spiritual cleansing is first and foremost. You will need two teaspoons of frankincense resin, a sprig of dried rosemary, charcoal briquettes, a heatproof container for the charcoal, and a lighting utensil. (Any local herb or Neopagan shop should have the herbs and resin regularly stocked.) Prepare this cleansing incense by placing two teaspoons of the frankincense resin in a container that allows for grinding (a mortar and pestle are perfect). Add two teaspoons of the dried rosemary. Mix and crush the frankincense and rosemary until the two are completely mixed in equal portions.

Go to your chosen spot with your supplies in hand. Clear and calm your mind. Let any tension flow away from your body. Take three deep breaths to clear your mind, body, and spirit. Place a charcoal briquette in a heatproof container and light it. Once the charcoal is glowing red, place a pinch of the incense onto the briquette.

Walk slowly around your chosen sacred space with the incense container in your hands. The smoke of the incense should fill the space completely. If you walk in a circle during the cleansing, then walk counterclockwise. Visualize all negative energy transforming into positive energy. Place more incense on the charcoal as needed.

After the space has been cleansed, it should feel light and pleasing. If you sense anything that seems "off" or awry, attempt the cleansing again. However, if the space continues to feel strange, try another area for your sacred space.

## Dragon Ritual Altar

While a formal altar is not necessary to commune with dragon energy, many magickal practitioners like to have an established "center" for their esoteric practice. Certainly, a ritual grows in power each time that it is performed. Likewise, an altar will also grow more powerful with each ritual. With time, the altar will become a potent conduit for your energy connection with the dragons. Together, the altar and sacred space will echo the dragon energy smoothly upon activation.

When choosing a dragon altar, make sure that it has at least one flat surface and is sturdy enough to safely hold burning objects, like candles and incense, as well as other ritual items. The altar need not be expensive or complicated; start with something simple.

Many esoteric practitioners place their altars in the north or east, typically wherever they recognize the earth element, in order to establish a solid foundation for energy work. For a dragon altar, it is recommended that the altar be placed within the earth element as well. Earth energy will ground the altar in a spiritual sense and give it an esoteric sturdiness. But it is a personal choice, of course.

## Altar Consecration

To attune the altar with dragon energy, use a simple consecration, much like we did with creating sacred space. Here is what you will need for the altar consecration:

- Dragon consecration oil, pre-mixed in bottle (see appendix A)
- Incense: Equal parts of dried rosemary and frankincense resin
- Incense burner and charcoal briquette

Take your mixed oil, incense, and incense supplies to your altar. Calm yourself and make sure that you are at peace. Light the incense and allow the smoke to cover the altar, both above and below. Once the altar has been touched by the smoke of the incense, place the incense burner on the altar. Take the dragon consecration oil and moisten the index finger of your dominant hand. Using the oil on your fingertip, write the word "Begin" upon the altar. Wait three breaths. With more oil on the same finger, write the word "Remember" upon the altar. Wait three breaths. Now write the word "Love" on the altar. Three more breaths. Finally, write the word "Mother" on the altar with the oil. Speak the words:

> *This altar is now consecrated and attuned to the dragons.*
> *I ask the ancient and mighty dragons to bless this space*
> *With their wisdom, power, and protection.*
> *So be it.*

Your personal dragon altar is now activated and functioning as a gateway for you to connect with the dragon realm. Whenever your energy work at the altar is concluded, close the gateway with these words:

*Ancient and Mighty Dragons,*
*Our work here has finished.*
*Stay if you will, go if you must.*
*Let there always be peace and trust between us.*
*So be it.*

For future workings at the altar, activate the gateway with candle, incense, or a word that is known only to you and the dragons. Whenever your work at the altar is concluded, be sure and close the gateway.

## Altar Energy Exercises

You should work with your dragon altar and sacred space often to empower it. Every time that you do energy work in this space, you and the space will become more attuned to each other's vibrations. As more time passes and more energy work is done, your ritual space will become a powerful source for communing with dragons.

The following energy work is suggested to enhance and empower your altar and sacred space:

### Altar Activation

Establish a daily routine of activating your altar. Go to your altar, stand before it, and take three deep breaths. Calm your mind and body. Place the fingertips of both hands on the altar. Concentrate on the connection between your flesh and the altar's surface. Imagine your hands beginning to glow with a light blue color. Allow that color to spread from your fingertips all across the altar, above and below it. Speak these words:

*I ask the ancient and mighty dragons to bless this space*
*with their wisdom, power, and protection.*
*So be it.*

### Meditation in Sacred Space

Meditate within your sacred space. Establish a routine (daily, if possible) of meditating for 20–30 minutes in your sacred space. Simply make yourself comfortable, close your eyes, and allow your mind, spirit, and body to just "be" in this space.

### Sacred Space and Altar Preservation

Maintain your altar and sacred space. Keep the altar clean and do not place non-ritual objects on it. Keep your sacred space clean and tidy as well. A messy ritual space creates barriers to energy flow. Make the cleaning a part of your esoteric dragon practice. Dedicate the cleaning to the dragons with a song or poem that you sing or recite as you clean.

### Enhance Your Sacred Space

Enhance your dragon altar and sacred space. It is not necessary, but if you are inspired to enhance your space and altar with statuary, symbols, or other ritual objects, by all means, do so. Working with dragon energy *should* inspire you.

## INITIATING YOUR CONNECTION TO DRAGONS

Building sacred space and a dragon altar within that space will open the gateway to communing with dragon energy, but what is communing with dragon energy like? What is the best way to prepare for this type of energy work? Those answers can only be found by making an energetic dragon connection. That being the case, a familiar dragon type is best chosen for the initial dragon energy connection. The guardian dragon is a good energy to call, as this archetype is well known, and most people have at least heard the tales of these dragons and thus already have a lore connection with them.

Fierce protectors of mounds of treasure, guardian dragons have a devotion to duty that is perhaps only surpassed by their alleged greed and stubbornness. Not all guardian dragons are defenders of riches and jewels, though. There were guardian dragons that were faithful watchers of temples and sites that were sacred to the gods of the ancient world. Hardly villains or creatures of evil, these dragons were respected and honored. None of these guardian dragons ever willingly abandoned their purpose; for hundreds, sometimes thousands, of years, they dutifully fulfilled their designation as stewards. As part of their own cycle of growth, guardian dragons do eventually transform. Their hoard or temple passes on to another keeper, and the dragon evolves. It is this type of guardian dragon with which we will first connect.

To prepare for communing with a guardian dragon's energy, I will first share what the experience of other humans has been when they encountered these archetypal dragons. We shall see that for both dragon and human, in both a physical and spiritual sense, a certain pattern of change emerges. There are motifs in the old tales that we can use as guideposts as we encounter the gateways on the path of seeking dragons. We can expect that by interacting with these dragons, a similar type of transformation will begin for the seeker as well. As we reexamine various selections of ancient dragon lore, the focus will be on both dragon *and seeker*. Here is the tale of the hero Jason of the Argonauts, seeker of the Golden Fleece, and the mighty guardian, the Colchian Dragon.

## Guardian Dragon Lore: Jason and Sowing the Dragon's Teeth

My first encounter with the motif of sowing the dragon's teeth was in the tale *Jason and the Argonauts*. In the Argonaut story, Jason is a young warrior who has a legitimate claim to the throne of the Greek kingdom of Iolcus, which had been taken violently by the then ruling king, Pelias. Pelias would not suffer any threats to his throne, so when Jason was born, Jason's mother faked a stillborn death and sent Jason away to be raised and tutored by the centaur Chiron.

As a young man, Jason makes his way back to Iolcus. Unfortunately for him, Pelias has been warned by an oracle and recognizes Jason for who he really is. When Jason unabashedly announces that he has arrived to claim the throne, Pelias sets a seemingly impossible task: Jason must obtain the Golden Fleece from the Garden of Ares where it is guarded by the sleepless (and enormous) dragon of Colchis. If Jason can bring the Golden Fleece back to Iolcus, Pelias promises to peacefully surrender his throne. Otherwise, Jason must take the throne by force.

Jason elects to pursue the Golden Fleece. He gathers quite the troop of Greek heroes; among them are Herakles, Atalanta, Orpheus, and Theseus. He is gifted a magickal ship, the *Argo*, and with the blessings and favor of the Greek goddesses Hera and Athena, Jason and the Argonauts set out for the kingdom of Colchis.

Upon their arrival in Colchis, Jason is very forthcoming with his purpose; he truthfully tells King Aeetes that he has come for the prized Golden Fleece. Aeetes, in turn, puts forth a challenge that he is sure will kill the young Greek and rid him of his foolish ambition: he tasks Jason with yoking a pair of fire-breathing bulls, plowing a field with them, and then planting a handful of dragon's teeth in the newly turned soil. If Jason can do this, the Golden Fleece will be given freely to him.

One of the basic concepts for any kind of growth is the placing of an object (a seed, perhaps) in a controlled environment and then tending that seed to initiate growth and change. With dragon interaction, it is no different. In this tale, Jason is planting dragon's teeth. He does not know what will happen, but he finds the courage to continue his heroic journey. After he successfully yokes the fire-breathing bulls, the field is plowed. Jason then plants the dragon's teeth.

To Jason's amazement, the dragon's teeth yield a crop of fully grown, fierce, and rather angry warriors. Jason knows that he probably cannot survive a battle with even one of them, and certainly not against all of them. Jason needs an ally.

Fortunately for Jason, the goddess Athena was still looking after him. She coaxed Eros, the god of passion, into shooting an arrow of love into the heart of King Aeetes's daughter. Eros's aim was true, and Medea was now deeply in love with the young Greek hero. She would become his guide through the upcoming dragon encounter and work her own deep magick to ensure her lover's success.

As Jason looks upon the warriors with trepidation, Medea, who has been aiding Jason, tells him to toss a large stone into their midst. Again, Jason is not quite sure of what will transpire, but he takes Medea's advice. She tells him not to worry, for the stone will cause the warriors to battle each other. When their ranks have been thinned to just a few, Jason is told to enter the fray and slay those that remain. Jason does exactly as Media says, and every warrior is vanquished.

King Aeetes is untrue to his promise and not quite ready to follow through with giving Jason the Golden Fleece. So Medea, still under the spell of Eros's love arow, determines to help Jason steal it. She decides to place a powerful sleep upon the guardian dragon. When the dragon is fast asleep, Jason climbs up the dragon's massive body and removes the fleece from the tree in which it hangs. Jason immediately flees Colchis as the dragon lies in slumber, taking Medea with him as she continues to skillfully work her magick for his success.

## Meaning within the Tale

On the surface, Jason's "sowing the dragon's teeth" is a simple story motif where a quest seeker takes the teeth of a dragon, plants those teeth in freshly tilled earth, and then has to deal with the results of the sowing. In modern times, "sowing the dragon's teeth" has become a metaphor to describe when an action will ultimately lead to conflict. Let us pause right here and look at this with a more discerning eye. Rather than chaos and conflict, perhaps "sowing the dragon's teeth" has deeper meaning. Might it be one of those hidden doorways that lead to the deep places where dragons dwell?

What is the symbolic interpretation of the sowing? For Jason, the planting of the dragon's teeth is akin to planting the seeds of chaos. When the warriors emerge, they do not immediately attack anyone or anything. They appear to have no focus or target; they simple "are." This is in alignment with the Greek meaning for the state of "chaos." Chaos is an abyss, the beginning, the primeval state of creation, that moment when all things are in motion and yet perfectly still, awaiting the influence that will direct the energy and its purpose.

This is not unlike the creation myths from many cultures where our own world is birthed from turbulent and dangerous energetic forces. The act of sowing the dragon's teeth can be seen as a microcosmic action that can and will ripple, sometimes violently, into this world and others.

For his interaction with the sowing of the dragon's teeth, Jason is advised to initiate destruction by Medea. She, for her part, is strongly influenced by her desire for Jason to survive, but she also comes from a lineage of powerful, magickal beings and most likely understands what is really going on with Jason and his "sowing the dragon's teeth." Medea is not only the daughter of the king, but also the granddaughter of Helios, the sun god. Moreover, Medea's aunt is Circe, a witch from *The Odyssey* who is a beguiler of Odysseus and his crew. Later, when Medea is in great need after having exacted cruel revenge upon Jason, her grandfather Helios sends a chariot pulled by two dragons to whisk her away to safety.

Following Medea's advice, Jason's management of the chaos, his facing of this abyss of turbulent potential, results first in fury and then the death of the sons of the dragon's teeth. This is an interesting outcome since Jason's planting of the dragon's teeth was meant as an impossible task. In fact, it was intended to kill him.

But, if it's true that worlds can be birthed from this same type of energy, then it follows that if the chaos is effectively manipulated in a proper manner, creation will be the result. The dragon's teeth and their power are a mystery in themselves. In Jason's tale, the dragon to whom the teeth belonged is not clearly identified or named. In fact, the only specific dragon in this tale is the guardian dragon who stands in sleepless watch over the fabled Golden Fleece—the dragon of Colchis.

Although Cadmus, from this book's introduction, and Jason had quite different experiences with sowing the teeth of the Ismenian Dragon, both of these men were deeply changed by the process. Cadmus used the dragon's teeth as the catalyst for founding a city, became a king, and finally transformed into a dragon. For Jason, the sons of the dragon's teeth were an obstacle, something that he had to remove in order to move forward with his quest for the Golden Fleece and ultimately claim his right to become a king.

The depth of Jason's transformation from this experience may best be illustrated on a vase painting from the fifth century BCE. Upon this vase, Jason is being devoured by the dragon of Colchis and then expelled from the dragon with Jason's body still intact and the hero very much alive.

Jason's path on this quest is frequently challenged, and each challenge comes with decisions that must be made. Each decision results in an action, and that action initiates immediate and profound change. As these changes take place, ripples from the pattern of transformation occur on many levels for the dragon seeker. Emotionally, the seeker must ride the tides of their reaction to change. Typically, we are resistant to change, even when we seek it willingly, and the storm of emotions can often lead to physical weariness and even mental fatigue. However, the discomfort of change can be smoothed and even overcome with spiritual practice and preparation. That is what this book, at its core, is about.

## MEDITATION: SEEKING THE DRAGON'S TEETH

Connecting and communing with the dragons, entwining their energy with your own, is "seeking dragons." Working at your altar or meditating with the dragons will allow you to be transformed. We will use the paths of those who have gone before us as a guide. In truth, as you read this text and experience dragon energy, you will be "sowing the dragon's teeth."

Locate a small area that is quiet and where you will not be disturbed. This can be outside or inside; the most important consideration for these meditations is that you are comfortable and feel safe. Be sure to wear clothing that does not hinder your movement and that the temperature and lighting are pleasant. Sit or lie down, whichever suits you, and close your eyes.

Breathe deeply. In and out. Concentrate on your breath as it enters your lungs, filling you with life, and then feel it exhale, leaving you energized.

Now, focus on one deep, slow breath to energize and clear your body. In and out. Another deep, slow breath to energize and clear your mind. In and out. Finally, another deep, slow breath to energize and clear your spirit.

Let the cares and concerns of the mundane world roll away from your neck… your shoulders… your arms… your fingers. Allow your back to relax, from your neck down, down, down to the base of your spine… and just breathe…

Allow your focus to rest behind your closed eyes as you feel your body relax completely. You are still. You are quiet.

In your mind's eye, see yourself on a rocky hillside. There are scatterings of dew-moistened grass. The air is clear and fresh. The sun is warm upon your face. The energy of this place, of this time, is solid, good, and strong.

You stand at the bottom slope of a tall, snow-crested mountain. As you look up, you see a path that leads up the mountain, but the way is not clear, and your eyes quickly lose the path in a gray haze.

Begin walking upon the mountain path, slowly, slowly, slowly ascending. Each footstep is deliberate and sure. Your breathing is deep and satisfying.

The haze appears to be fog or perhaps clouds. In the distance, you can hear the crashing of waves, and you immediately smell the brine of the sea. The air is damp but not chilled, and it looks as if the fog is clearing just ahead of you.

Continue walking upon the mountain path, slowly, slowly, slowly ascending. Each footstep is deliberate and sure. Your breathing is deep and satisfying.

The mountain shakes and rumbles, causing you to pause. Above you, storm clouds gather. You feel the need to find shelter until the storm passes.

Take a few more steps and you will see a cave entrance in the mountain. The way is dark and still. Yet, it is shelter from the coming storm.

Take a deep breath and enter the cave.

As soon as you are inside, you feel calm and safe. You sit down quietly, not too far from the entrance, and wait for the storm to pass.

With your hands, feel the ground beneath you. Is it stone? Sand or dirt? How does the cave smell? Is the air damp or dry? Is there water anywhere nearby that you can hear? Let your senses fully awaken.

Take three deep breaths.

You hear the unmistakable sound of gently running water.

Take three deep breaths.

You hear a distant rumble. In your mind's eye, you see a dragon … a massive creature that is lying peacefully near a running stream. The dragon raises its head, flicks its tongue, and then turns its gaze upon you.

*This place is sacred, and I am its guardian.*
*Speak your name and declare why you have come.*

Bow your head and send your name silently to the guardian dragon. Tell the guardian that you seek to learn the wisdom of the dragons.

The dragon continues to study you, its gaze piercing and unblinking.

*You have been shown the path to this place, but now you must prove yourself worthy of such knowledge and wisdom. Henceforth, I shall observe your deeds with more interest. I will weigh your words carefully. Listen! You know this place and shall return, but do not venture elsewhere until I have shown you! You must prove trustworthy, and your heart must prove true. Go now and remember!*

Take three more deep breaths. Concentrate on the back of your closed eyes. With your next breath, you feel a shift in the energy around you. You begin to feel a bit heavier as you become aware of your body.

When you open your eyes, you will have returned to your safe and sacred space in this world. You will feel refreshed by this communion with the dragons.

Now, one more deep breath … and open your eyes.

## DRAGON JOURNALING

If you already keep a journal, you can simply add the entries from this book in that same journal. If you do not already have a journal, I highly recommend that you at least keep one as you read this text and record not only your responses to the meditations but also your experiences outside of the meditations. This could include dreams, "eureka" moments, or whatever you feel is important to remember. You need not write paragraph upon paragraph; simple words, drawings, or short descriptions will suffice. I have found that journals are especially useful for reading weeks, months, or years later and identifying patterns in your experiences, dreams, and meditations.

## JOURNAL ENTRIES

For this first meditation, the following journal entries are suggested:

1. Describe the experience of your senses in the cave. What did you feel? What did you smell? What did you hear?

2. Describe or sketch the guardian dragon and its spring of running water. Do you imagine that the water is cold or tepid? Would it taste salty or sweet? What color is the dragon? What color are its eyes? Is it winged?

3. Write a note to the guardian dragon wherein you describe why you wish to learn and commune with the dragons.

## THE CALL OF THE DRAGON OVERVIEW

In this chapter, the foundation for working with dragon energy was established. Using sacred space and a dragon altar as focus tools, the experience of spiritual transformation has been initiated. Investigating the transformative tale of the Colchian Dragon as more than a mere "dragon slayer" story created a new energetic connection to this guardian dragon. Then, in meditation with a guardian dragon, yet another energetic connection to dragons was established. Take some time to reflect on these experiences. If you want, experience the first meditation again. Use your journal to document each visit to the cave as well as any insights that may come to you.

## CHAPTER THREE

# DRAGONS AND TRANSFORMATION

In the vast collection of dragon lore, you will consistently observe that dragons and those who interact with them experience a profound metamorphosis: simply put, they—the dragon and those with whom they interact—*transform*.

From a magickal practitioner's perspective, seeking dragons is synonymous with seeking spiritual growth. It is an attempt to evolve our innermost being and higher spiritual self. This is what it means to learn the wisdom of the dragons: to transform ourselves. In doing so, something—perhaps even everything—about us and our view of the world will change.

## HUMAN TO DRAGON:
## DRAGON SLAYERS TRANSFORMED

Another look at the story of *Cadmus and Harmonia* sheds more light on transformation via human interaction with a dragon. Many years after slaying the Ismenian Dragon, Cadmus, king of Thebes and renowned dragon slayer, is heavily burdened with guilt and discontent. As the end of his life approaches, he is nearly broken from the great tragedies over the many years, and he is weary of living in the violent world of humans. Through all these years, one worry in particular has gnawed at him: he wonders if the slaying of the Ismenian Dragon was the mistake that cursed his life.

Unable to stay in the city that he founded, Thebes, Cadmus and his wife, Harmonia, began to wander the world. His doubt continued to devour his innermost being. Finally, in despair, he voices his anguish. As his words and pain mingle in an outpouring of grief, the gods hear him and answer. Then and there, Cadmus and his wife are transformed into small serpents.[8]

Why would Cadmus and his wife be changed into dragons? Was this a punishment or a reward? Could it have been an expected transformation, or was this a wild result? At first glance, it might well seem that Cadmus is being punished, but if that is true, the punishment seems long overdue, and why would Harmonia be punished as well?

From an esoteric perspective, it seems more likely that the words spoken by Cadmus, a release of sound and emotion akin to a prayer of desperation, are a *trigger* for a process that transforms him and his wife into serpents. Consider that sound and emotion are used to connect to and move energy in common spiritual practice. From singing hymns to chanting mantras to voicing the *om* of the universe, sound is used as a powerful conduit for spiritual connection and energy movement. In esoteric practice, spiritual connection and energetic movement are what is commonly referred to as *magick*. I will go into more detail about dragon magick in chapter 4, "Dragon Energy and

---

8. Ovid, "Book 4," n.p.

Elemental Dragons," but for now, consider that Cadmus's transformation was less a punishment and more of an intended result.

Might it be that this type of dragon transformation is a milestone in the spiritual and physical path of a "dragon slayer"? Consider that Cadmus might have been carrying the energy and spirit of the Ismenian Dragon inside of him for all those years. This dragon energy was swirling and growing inside of him. Cadmus was becoming a dragon. The slaying of the Ismenian Dragon was the beginning of deep transformation for Cadmus.

Another dragon tale where a human becomes a dragon is the Scandinavian story of Sigurd and the slaying of the dragon Fafnir. The episode is well-known, but the story of Fafnir's origins is often ignored or passes so quickly that it can easily be dismissed. Yet, here is another illustration of human to dragon transformation.

Fafnir was a dwarven prince, the son of King Hreidmar. He had two brothers, Otr and Regin. Some of their family were gifted with the magickal ability to shapeshift. Tragically, Otr is killed and skinned while he is in the form of an otter. In turn, King Hreidmar demands a *wergild*, or "man-price," be paid by his killer. He names the price of enough gold to fill and cover the dead otter's fur.

The wergild is paid in full and more: Hreidmar becomes the proud owner of a massive mound of gold, jewels, and treasures. Unfortunately, the gold and jewels are cursed and thus begins a cycle of greed and betrayal.

Regin and Fafnir both feel that they should have a share of the hoard. Hreidmar disagrees and declares that he will keep it all. Angry, Fafnir then slays his father as the king sleeps and banishes Regin to the wilds.[9]

To better guard his enormous prize, Fafnir then begins the process of shapeshifting into a mighty dragon. The tales are not specific as to how he manages such a complicated transmutation, but it does seem to involve a magickal spell or object named the *Ægishjálmr*, or the Helm of Awe. (The Helm of Awe is a rune spell, which is explained in more detail in appendix B.)

---

9. J. R. R. Tolkien, *The Legend of Sigurd and Gudrún*, ed. Christopher Tolkien (New York: Houghton Mifflin Harcourt, 2009), 66–71, 99–104.

The magick of shapeshifting is complex, but with Fafnir, we have a dragon that is a master of this power. Having that tidbit of knowledge, we now have an awareness that as we seek to commune and interact with dragons, we may well meet them in *other* forms.

Fafnir continues to evolve in his dragon shape; when we see him again when Sigurd challenges him, we see that even in death, the magick of a dragon is still quite potent.

## DRAGONS WHO TRANSFORM THE WORLD

Dragons can also be found as physical parts of our world: lakes, rivers, oceans, mountains, and even the earth itself. The ancient and mighty dragon Tiamat is front and center of a creation myth from ancient Babylonia. Tiamat, like Fafnir, was a shapeshifter.

She was also called *Ummu-Hubur*, "who formed all things." During a mighty battle between the Babylonian gods, Tiamat is slain, and her corpse torn in half. One half of her becomes the earth and all things on it; the other half becomes the sky.

From this we learn that the earth beneath our feet and the sky above us, the very air that we breathe, are parts of a great dragon energy that pulses and flows all around us. To connect with the grass, trees, wind—with everything—is to connect with dragon energy.

One of the more beautiful tales of dragon transformation is where the dragon is reborn as a constellation. Stars have a much, much higher vibration than we do. Hence, the transformation of a physical dragon into a brilliant formation of dazzling, celestial energy can certainly be seen as a liberating and progressive spiritual evolution.

The constellation Draco has been recognized by many cultures. It is the eighth largest constellation, and though it is only visible in the Northern Hemisphere, it is never absent from the night sky. The Greeks believed that Draco was formed after Hera's beloved dragon, Ladon, was slain. Ladon was a guardian of the Golden Apples. The half-god Herakles must steal them, and he must figure out a way to either persuade the dragon to give them up or slay it. Herakles, in most versions, chooses the latter. Hera mourns Ladon's sacrifice and determines to honor him by placing his spirit into the sky in the form of what we now call the constellation Draco. In ancient Rome, it was Minerva who defeated the dragon and then tossed it to the stars where it formed into the Draco arrangement.[10]

In many modern Neopagan practices, an awareness of and connection with the energy of celestial objects is a familiar concept. The sun and moon are quite often the focal point of many modern rituals, and let us not forget the layperson who simply consults the horoscope section on a regular basis. With that in mind, connecting with star energy can be seen as another approach to esoteric ritual and practice.

## ENERGY EXERCISES

Understanding the concept of transformation, especially spiritual transformation, requires observation and experience. Accepting and allowing spiritual transformation for yourself can sometimes lead to brief periods of uncomfortable change. To smooth and ease the transformation process, the following energy work is suggested as an aid in recognizing and experiencing transformation.

### Photo Meditation

Gather some pictures of yourself from various ages of your life. Go to your altar and activate it as explained in chapter 2. Place the pictures on the altar, images facing up, in no particular pattern or order. Clear your mind and calm yourself. Pick up each picture and study the image. Note facial expressions, body positions, and environments. Place the pictures back on the altar in order of your age in the image, youngest to oldest. Take the pictures where you are the youngest and oldest and place them side by side. From youth to maturity, much has changed for you: your appearance, your dreams, your passions—to name a few. Try and remember back to your earliest memories. Take note of how the passage of time has changed from your perspective as a child to an adult. Do you feel wiser? More connected?

---

10. Kim Ann Zimmermann, "Draco Constellation: Facts About the Dragon," Space, Future US Inc., July 20, 2017, https://www.space.com/16755-draco-constellation.html.

**Mantra**

Use this phrase, "The only thing for certain is change," as a daily affirmation. Accepting and becoming comfortable—even eager—for change to occur is one of the keys to mastering any fear that you might have of transformation and change. When you find that you are dreading something new or different, repeat the phrase quietly in your mind (or aloud if you have the privacy) and remember to concentrate on your breathing.

# MEDITATION:
# CONNECTING TO DRACO, STAR DRAGON

With a focus on an energetic connection with dragons, you will use what you have learned in this chapter in a meditation. Specifically, this meditation is an attempt to spiritually and energetically reach out and connect with the star energy of the dragon Ladon, who is now called Draco.

Locate an area that is quiet and where you will not be disturbed. This can be outside or inside; the most important consideration for these meditations is that you are comfortable and feel safe. Be sure to wear clothing that does not hinder your movement and that the temperature and lighting are pleasant. Sit or lie down, whichever suits you, and close your eyes.

Breathe deeply. In and out. Concentrate on your breath as it enters your lungs, filling you with life, and then feel it exhale, leaving you energized.

Now, focus on one deep, slow breath to energize and clear your body. In and out. Another deep, slow breath to energize and clear your mind. In and out. Finally, another deep, slow breath to energize and clear your spirit.

Let the cares and concerns of the mundane world roll away from your neck … your shoulders … your arms … your fingers. Allow your back to relax, from your neck down, down, down to the base of your spine … and just breathe …

Allow your focus to rest behind your closed eyes as you feel your body relax completely. You are still. You are quiet.

In your mind's eye, see yourself on a rocky hillside. There are scatterings of dew-moistened grass. The air is clear and fresh. The sun is warm upon your face. The energy of this place, of this time, is solid, good, and strong.

You stand at the bottom slope of a tall, snow-crested mountain. As you look up, you see a path that leads up the mountain; it is a path that is becoming more familiar to you.

Begin walking upon the mountain path, slowly, slowly, slowly ascending. Each footstep is deliberate and sure. Your breathing is deep and satisfying.

Take a few more steps and you will see a cave entrance in the mountain. Take a deep breath and enter the cave.

As soon as you are inside, take a quiet moment. With your hands, feel the ground beneath you. What do you smell? Is the air damp or dry? What can you hear? Take the time to let your senses fully awaken.

Take three deep breaths and close your eyes.

You feel a shift in the energy around you, a slight nudge, and you sense a gentle darkness descend.

Open your eyes.

You are now standing upon the side of the mountain. To the south, a wine-red ocean dances slowly as it kisses a far shore. Above you stretches a brilliant night sky. There is no moon and no other light…save the dazzling light of the silver stars.

Now, turn to the north. Search for the brightest star and with your inner voice call out to Draco:

*Mighty Draco! Silver lord and star dragon!*
*I, [your name], call to you!*
*Sing your story.*
*Share your wisdom.*
*Shine on, Silver One!*

Continue staring at the stars with your mind's eye. Allow your inner vision to relax its focus. Watch as each star's light reaches out and touches the light of the other stars. See the stars form the great Greek dragon Ladon, now called Draco, beloved guardian of Hera, goddess and queen of Olympus.

Hear the dragon's voice like a clear bell upon the gentle om of the universe as the stars and planets gently ebb and flow. Allow your spirit to join in with this rhythm. Allow your breath to mingle with the energy of the universe as you begin to form the sound "Om." Take a deep, deep breath. Hold the breath. With your inner voice, physical voice, or both, begin the "Oh" sound from deep in your chest. Exhale gently as the "Oh" sound forms.

*Oohhhhhhhhhhh*

Hold the "Oh" and continue to gently exhale as you allow the sound to move up through your throat, and just before it enters your mouth, begin the "M" sound.

*Mmmmmmmmmmmm*

Hold the "M" sound until your breath has been completely exhaled, close your mouth, and gently settle again into silence.

Repeat the "Om" breath until you feel that you are fully relaxed and vibrating with the stars.

Now, look again to the stars of Draco. Visualize your energy touching and mingling with the light from those stars.

Quiet your mind and listen … allow Draco to speak to you … this message is only for you …

When the dragon's voice has silenced, take three more deep breaths.

Concentrate on the back of your closed eyes. Feel the weight of your hands. Your feet. Feel the beating of your heart. With your next breath, you feel a shift in the energy around you. You begin to feel a bit heavier as you become more aware of your body. Now, slowly open your eyes.

When you open your eyes, you will have returned to your safe and sacred space in this world. You feel refreshed by this communion with the dragons.

## JOURNAL ENTRIES

For this meditation, the following journal entries are suggested:

1. Be sure to record what Draco or any other star dragons said to you during the meditation. Draw any symbols or numbers that might have appeared.

2. Describe the dragon's voice with as much detail as you can remember. Use color and vibration, such as "The dragon's voice seemed to be silver with a tinge of electric blue" and "The dragon's voice was slow and deliberate" or "quick and spirited."

3. Did you see other dragon constellations in the night sky during the meditation? Describe what you saw and what you see now, in the physical world, as you gaze up at Draco or other constellations of stars.

## TRANSFORMATION OVERVIEW

In this chapter, through careful reading of dragon lore, you have seen that dragons and those with whom they interact *transform*. Sowing the dragon's teeth is synonymous with seeking spiritual growth. In seeking dragons, seek to mature your innermost being. *Transformation* is what it means to heed and learn the wisdom of the dragons: these spiritual metamorphoses change everything about us and our view of the world.

If you wish, experience the meditations again. Use your journal to document each visit. The next chapter delves into the realms of energy and elemental dragons.

## CHAPTER FOUR

---

# DRAGON ENERGY
# AND ELEMENTAL DRAGONS

To find and experience the energy of dragons, you need only step outside. Many of the oldest creation tales reveal that the lakes, rivers, oceans, mountains, rocks—in fact, the entire earth itself—were all crafted from ancient and mighty dragons. Some areas of our earth are more potent with dragon energy than others, but let us begin with an overview of energy and what it is.

## DRAGON ENERGY

What is energy? How do you connect with energy? *Energy*, as used in this text, is synonymous with electromagnetic energy, which is "a form of energy that can be reflected or emitted from objects through electrical or magnetic waves."[11] Electromagnetic frequencies, or EMFs, surround us. Some EMF sources in our everyday life are X-rays, microwaves, radio waves, and even sunlight. Not all EMFs can be experienced via the five "usual" senses of sight, sound, touch, taste, or smell, though. For instance, the earth's magnetic field is an EMF, yet we do not experience this energy through our normal senses.

In my personal tradition of esoteric practice (and my esoteric group is not the only one to teach and practice this concept), we believe that humans also have an EMF that surrounds us. In fact, we believe that this energy surrounds all things on this planet. To connect with energy means to intertwine your personal energy with the energy of something other than yourself.

As you may surmise, intertwining your own personal energy with anything should be done with an abundance of caution. It is a good and safe esoteric practice to be very sure of what and with whom you are energetically connecting. This text will provide several methods for safely connecting with dragon and earth energy.

## HOLDING THE TENSION

*Holding the tension*, in its most simple form, means reaching a comfortable balance between two things. Imagine sitting on a seesaw with a human partner. Rather than going up and down, try to achieve a state of stillness for the seesaw by balancing the two ends. It may take a few tries as you test various positions, both for the seesaw and for the occupants. You can find the balance, though, and when you do, concentrate on holding it as long as you can. This is *holding the tension* in a physical sense.

In an esoteric dragon practice, *holding the tension* means balancing your personal energy (the energy that you put into a ritual or spell) with the energy of the dragons with whom you ally. The energy shared in between should be

---

11. "What Is Electromagnetic Energy?" Reference, Ask Media Group, LLC., March 29, 2020, https://www.reference.com/science-technology/electromagnetic-energy-118c0f3e43f35ef.

sensed and regulated so that a comfortable balance is achieved. Like with the seesaw exercise, finding the energy balance may require adjusted positioning of your body or of other physical objects. It may require a certain time or place to achieve the balance.

## DRAGON LINES

In addition to the earth's magnetic field, there are also lines of concentrated energy that appear to run just below the earth's surface. These streams of energy are called *ley lines* or *dragon lines*. This is not a scientific statement, mind you, but it is a theory that has been proposed and accepted by some esoteric practitioners.

Ley lines are also used to explain what appears to be the positioning of certain sites of worship. For example, in England, the sites of Glastonbury Tor, Stonehenge, and Avebury are proposed to all be connected by a triangular flow of earth energy.[12] As it relates to energy work, these ley lines can be viewed as powerful flows of dragon energy. When you feel the sturdy earth beneath your feet, you are feeling the energy of the earth dragons. When you draw breath and look in wonder at the sky above you, you are sensing the power of the air dragons. When you feel the cool waters of a mountain stream, you are feeling the essence of the water dragons. As you are warmed by the embers of a soothing fire, you are feeling the energy of a fire dragon. All of this and more is part of the great dragon energy that pulses and flows everywhere. Simply put, to connect with the natural world is to connect with dragon energy.

## ELEMENTAL DRAGONS

The energy of our natural world is shaped and formed by the sacred elements. These elements were recognized by the ancient world and are used by many modern esoteric practitioners today. These sacred elements can and do manifest into elemental dragons. The five elemental dragon types that we

---

12. Simon Ingram, "What Makes Glastonbury so Mystical," National Geographic, updated 14 May 2021, https://www.nationalgeographic.co.uk/history-and-civilisation/2019/06/what -makes-glastonbury-so-mystical; Joanne Pearson, *A Popular Dictionary of Paganism* (New York: RoutledgeCurzon, 2002), 67.

will study are synonymous with these sacred elements: earth, fire, water, air, and spirit. The Northern European magickal traditions also include ice as a sacred element. We will delve more deeply into the sacred element of ice in chapter 10.

All dragons are composed of the five sacred elements, but an elemental dragon is able to focus their energy on a specific element. An elemental dragon's color, sound, and energetic vibration are determined by their elemental alignment. The table here is intended to be a reference guide for the color spectrum, vibration, and sound of elemental dragons.

| Elemental Dragon | Earth Dragon | Fire Dragon | Water Dragon | Air Dragon | Spirit Dragon |
|---|---|---|---|---|---|
| Color Spectrum | Green | Red | Blue | Yellow | Purple |
| Slow Vibration | Forest green to deep brown | Dark red to purple | Indigo blue to navy | Gold to burnt yellow | Dark purple |
| Medium Vibration | Sandy brown to light green | Slight red to bright red | Ocean blue to sky blue | Flaxen to lemon yellow | Reddish-purple |
| High Vibration | Gray | Bright red to orange | Turquoise | Pale yellow | Violet |
| Sound | M | AH | E | I | OM |

*Elemental Dragon Correspondences*

## Earth Dragons

The amazing and varied geographical formations and landscapes of our planet are a physical manifestation of the earth dragon energy. Earth energy in general is slow and steady, and you can expect to feel that when you connect with earth dragon spirits. We can prepare for that connection with simple practice.

How does an earth dragon's energy feel? Try picking up a small rock in your hand. Close your eyes and concentrate on how this piece of the earth feels within your grasp. Then pick up a small tree branch and place it in your free hand. Concentrate on the rock and the branch. Allow the objects to move around by tilting your hands slightly. Note how each object responds to the change in angle. Gently squeeze your hands until the rock and branch are fully encircled by your flesh. Clear your mind. Be silent. Hear the distant heartbeat of the earth and allow it to become louder. Feel the slow, steady vibration in the rock and branch. This is earth dragon energy.

The earth dragon's vibration is solid and firm. These dragons are not obligated nor are they inclined to do anything quickly or with haste. Yet, because of their slow energetic vibration, these are the dragons that are the most approachable. Be aware, though, that interaction with them requires patience on a scale that is seldom practiced by humans. Hence, it is advised that you experience the deep earth energies on a regular basis. Take frequent quiet walks in the woods. Sit outside in a quiet place. Use your hands to touch the trees; use your bare feet to connect with the ground.

Earth dragons manifest in the physical world within the spectrum of green and vibrate with the rhythm of the earth, which surrounds where they have chosen to dwell. A dragon who lives in the loam and dirt of the earth moves through its domain much like an earthworm. It can be coaxed above ground when it rains, but these dragons prefer to slumber in the rich, damp soil. Likewise, a dragon who lives in a mountain has a dark and shadowy energy; they seldom move or utter any sound. Like the rock that they call home, mountain dragons are fixed and sturdy.

Look for earth dragons in landscapes that are undisturbed by humans. Sit upon the earth and still your mind. Listen for their voices in the damp soil; hear them in the rumble of the earth when it shakes. Know that these dragons may appear as tiny as a rock or as large as a mountain. Remember to practice patience; do not expect an earth dragon to immediately manifest when you first reach out to them. Consistent meditations will help to build trust. With time, you may just be rewarded with the friendship and alliance of an earth dragon.

## Fire Dragons

Fire dragons manifest in the physical world within the color spectrum of red and vibrate within the range of the alchemical process of heat transformation. Like the fires of a metalworker's forge, the potency (and approachability) of a fire dragon's energy can be gauged by the dragon's color. Brownish-red dragons have a slow vibration that is pleasantly warm. As the red becomes brighter and changes to orange, the dragon's vibration increases, as does their physical heat.

Fire energy is much swifter than earth energy; in its physical form, such as with burning wood or a lava flow, fire energy can move at a rapid pace as it grows in heat and size. A fire dragon's energy is intense. Like a physical burning, you must be mindful and respectful of this energy when attempting to connect with it.

The fire dragon's vibration is usually quick and lithe. These dragons dance when they move; they are an energetic compilation of the intense heat from which they manifest. Interacting with their energy requires precautions for our physical selves. We must also learn and hone the ability to quickly heed their messages, which come in bursts of heat and flame.

To commune with fire dragons, you should first become comfortable with the element of fire itself. To do this, utilize a home fireplace or an out-door firepit if possible. Sit in a quiet place. Light your fire. Concentrate on how your body feels as it becomes warmed by the flames. Stare into the fire and still your mind. Slow your breathing and let your muscles relax. Know and respect that fire can indeed be dangerous, but when managed properly, it is a powerfully soothing energy source.

Once you are comfortable with the physical element of fire, you should connect with fire dragons by reaching out to the dragons of the lower vibrations first. When invited, fire dragons will readily dance in the flames, but they will also manifest with a slower and more approachable vibration in the embers from a wood or coal fire. It is these slower dragons that we will interact with first.

Begin by building and setting alight a small wood fire. Be sure to build the fire in a safe place, such as an outdoor firepit (have a fire extinguisher close by) and wear clothing that will not drape into the flames or become too warm. Light the fire and make yourself comfortable. Clear your mind. Be silent. Watch the flames as they move and consume the wood. Hear the sizzle of the flames. Feel the vibration in you as the warmth from the fire reaches your physical body. As the fire dies down, take a fire poker (or other safe tool) and slowly stir the coals.

Look for fire dragons to form in the coals as the colors shift and stir. Listen for their voices in the sizzling heat; hear them in the pop and hiss of the wood. Know that these dragons may appear as one tiny ember or as a massive flow of lava from a volcano. Their messages do not linger; they will disappear quickly, not unlike the element in which they manifest. Fire offerings of herbs or incense and regular communions will help to build trust with these elusive creatures. In time, you will learn how to translate their messages and forge a strong bond with the fire dragons.

## Water Dragons

Water dragons manifest within the spectrum of blue, and their vibration is set by the power of their chosen watery home. Water energy can be both swift and still. A churning ocean that is being fed by a storm has very active water dragons within it, and those dragons are moving fast and with tremendous power. Gentle streams and still waters are the homes of quieter water dragons. These are the dragon spirits easiest for a human to interact with.

Communing with water dragons does require proper preparation so that you are comfortable with the energy and thus able to hear their messages more clearly. To commune with water dragons, it is not required to physically enter a body of water. Certainly, immersing yourself safely into the water is a superb way to experience the water dragon energy. But if this is not possible, seating yourself near the water will do.

Find a spot near a still body of water or a gently flowing stream (a fountain or similar watery flow can suffice). Sit yourself comfortably. Observe the surface of the water. Slow your breathing and let your muscles relax. Listen to the water as it gently laps the shore or how it gurgles when it passes over a rock or log and the sigh as it releases and continues on its way. If you can, touch the water's surface with your hand. Slowly immerse your hand until it is covered with the water. Feel the slight resistance against your flesh. Adjust the position of your hand until you feel that it is in balance with the water. Concentrate on the slight push and pull within the water where your hand now rests. This is *holding the tension* with water energy. It takes practice and patience to learn how to reach and maintain the balance point between your hand and the water. It is the same between your energy and that of the spiritual world. This balance, physical and energetic, is what allows us to connect with the spiritual world.

Once you have spent some time practicing *holding the tension* with water, you are ready to connect with the lower vibratory water dragons. Look for most water dragons to appear just below the surface of the water. Listen for their voices as the water responds to movements. Know that these dragons may be as small as a drop of rain or as large as a mountain lake. Like the fire dragons, the water dragon messages do not linger; they will disappear quickly. Consistent visits to the abode of water dragons will help to establish trust with them. With patience and persistence, you will hear their messages and form a fast friendship with these wonderful creatures.

## Air Dragons

Dragons of the air manifest within the color spectrum of yellow. Their vibration is determined by the condition of the air in which they form. Air dragons that form from gentle winds are the easiest for humans to interact with. Dragons that manifest from the energy of storm winds or gales should be approached with a great deal of respect and an overabundance of caution.

As with the other elemental dragons, communing with air dragons requires preparation and practice with their element of air. When the wind is gentle and weather allows, go outside (or open a window) and find a comfortable place where you can feel the breeze. Slow your breathing and let your muscles relax. Listen to the air as it whistles through the leaves; hear its song as it races in the sky. Hold out your hand and feel the wind envelope your flesh. Like with the flowing water, concentrate on the resistance, this time between your hand and the wind. Move your hand until you feel that it is neither resisting nor being controlled by the wind. When you feel the point of balance, *hold the tension* between your hand and the wind and focus on the energetic exchange.

After you have spent some time *holding the tension* with the element of air, you are ready to connect with the lower vibratory air dragons. Look for air dragons to appear as the wind blows through and around the leaves of a tree, into and out of an opening in a rock, and in the swirling sands of the shore.

Listen carefully for their messages in the form of a whispery song. Know that the air dragons may be small enough to alight on your shoulder or large enough to fill the sky. Their songs can be lengthy compositions that are then learned and sung by other air dragons. Singing with them is a wonderful way to commune with these dragons. In time, you will come to recognize their songs and be able to easily visit with these delightful beings.

## Spirit Dragons

Spirit dragons are remarkable in that they are beautiful fusions of earth, fire, water, and air. These dragons manifest within the color spectrum of purple. The slower vibratory spirit dragons appear as dark purple, almost black, with a distinctive silver glow around their eyes. Medium vibratory spirit dragons manifest as reddish-purple with a red glow in their eyes. The fastest vibration for spirit dragons appears as a violet color with matching violet eyes.

Spirit dragons can only manifest when there are elemental dragons, at least one of each element, already present and active. That being the case, it would be best to find a place where the elements all meet and attempt communion with a spirit dragon at this location. This is probably easiest to do outside in a secluded place where a body of water meets the shore. Here, you have a place where the energies of air, earth, and water all naturally converge.

To add the element of fire to this convergence point, simply (and safely) build a fire or light a candle. Make yourself comfortable and relax. Allow your eyes to un-focus and awaken your other senses. Imagine an earth dragon forming nearby, followed by a fire dragon dancing in the flames, then a water dragon swimming near the shore as an air dragon flies just overhead.

Feel the four elements touching each other and join in an energetic burst of color and sound. Look for a spirit dragon to form first in the outer glow of the flames. As the combined energy grows in strength, the spirit dragon's color will slowly transform into a deep purple.

Let the spirit dragon reach out first. You may feel a tingle, both physically and energetically, as the spirit dragon gently touches the outer edge of your personal energy field. Their messages will come directly to your mind, sometimes as an image or a sound, and are for you only.

## ENERGY EXERCISES

Work with the dragons of earth, fire, water, air, and spirit, separately and together, as often as you can. A strong kinship with the elemental dragons will allow you, as a dragon practitioner, to ally with them more readily for your energy work. For example, calling rain will be much easier with water dragon allies; energy work for safe travel on a plane will be more effective with air dragon cooperation.

The following energy exercises are suggested to enhance and empower your relationship with the elemental dragons.

### Connecting with Earth Dragons: Dragon's Nest Creation

Make a permanent nest for when earth dragons visit your sacred space. Procure or make a basket (size is up to you—smaller will work just as well as larger) with straw or bedding. Go to your altar and activate it. Speak these words:

> *I make a safe place here for the earth dragons.*
> *Here may you find rest and respite upon your journeys.*
> *Stay for as long as you like.*
> *Depart when you must.*
> *Let there always be trust between us.*

Place the dragon nest in the area of your sacred space where you work with the earth dragons, usually east or north. Keep the bedding tidy and the area clean and welcoming.

### Connecting with Fire Dragons

For fire energy work, get a red, yellow, or orange candle. Go to your altar and place the candle on it. Light the candle. Make yourself comfortable. Stare into the candle flame and clear your mind of trouble. Meditate on the fire elementals. Do this daily, if possible, for 5–10 minutes.

**Connecting with Water Dragons**

For water energy work, take a vessel (cup or bowl) and fill it with clean water. If you have a small water fountain that can be powered at your altar, then it will work quite well for this exercise. Take the vessel of water or water fountain and place it on your altar. Make yourself comfortable. Place your fingertips into the water. Close your eyes and concentrate on the sensation of the water flowing around your flesh. Focus on being a part of the flow, not a blockage or deterrent. Do this daily, if possible, for 5–10 minutes.

**Connecting with Air Dragons**

For air energy work, get an incense burner and incense or stick incense, either will work. Go to your altar and light the incense. Make yourself comfortable. Watch the smoke of the incense rise into the air. Meditate on the air dragons as you place your hands into the incense smoke. Do this daily, if possible, for 5–10 minutes.

## MEDITATION: CONNECTING TO THE DRAGONS OF THE SACRED ELEMENTS

Continue to practice *holding the tension* with the elements and communing with the elemental dragons. When you feel that you are ready to make an even stronger connection to these dragons, add the following meditation to your dragon practice. Dragons of the Sacred Elements is designed to lead you even more deeply into the energy and mystery of the elemental dragons.

Locate an area that is quiet and where you will not be disturbed. This can be outside or inside; the most important consideration for these meditations is that you are comfortable and feel safe. Be sure to wear clothing that does not hinder your movement and that the temperature and lighting are pleasant. Sit or lie down, whichever suits you, and close your eyes.

Breathe deeply. In and out. Concentrate on your breath as it enters your lungs, filling you with life, and then feel it exhale, leaving you energized.

Now, focus on one deep, slow breath to energize and clear your body. In and out. Another deep, slow breath to energize and clear your mind. In and out. Finally, another deep, slow breath to energize and clear your spirit.

Let the cares and concerns of the mundane world roll away from your neck... your shoulders... your arms... your fingers. Allow your back to relax, from your neck down, down, down to the base of your spine... and just breathe...

Allow your focus to rest behind your closed eyes as you feel your body relax completely. You are still. You are quiet.

In your mind's eye, see yourself on a rocky hillside. There are scatterings of dew-moistened grass. The air is clear and fresh. The sun is warm upon your face. The energy of this place, of this time, is solid, good, and strong.

You stand at the bottom slope of a tall, snow-crested mountain. As you look up, you see a path that leads up the mountain; it is a path that is becoming more familiar to you.

Begin walking upon the mountain path, slowly, slowly, slowly ascending. Each footstep is deliberate and sure. Your breathing is deep and satisfying.

Take a few more steps and you will see a cave entrance in the mountain.

Take a deep breath and enter the cave.

You immediately feel a heavy stillness within the inky black cave. Within that stillness, you also sense an expectation. There is a bright flash of silver light that illuminates the cave for a few moments. As the darkness settles, in the eastern quadrant of the cave, you see pulsing orbs of green light. The lights dance for a few moments and then join to form the outline of a winged dragon.

As the dragon manifests, you can see her scales are interwoven with leaves and branches. Her claws and teeth shine like smooth granite. When she extends her wings, you see the moss and loam from the deep earth. The dragon settles into a quiet stance, her watchful gaze upon you.

With your inner voice, greet the earth dragon with this message:

*Hail, Dragon of Earth!*
*You, who form the mighty mountain,*
*Majestic and strong.*

*You, who slumber in the deep places,*
*Holding together the sinews of our world.*
*I, [your name], greet you in peace.*

The earth dragon nods at you and closes her eyes. A deep "M" sound begins to fill the cave.

There is a second flash. This time, the flash is a reddish-orange light. In the southern quadrant of the cave, you see small flames of red. The flames dance for a few moments and then join to form the outline of a fiery, winged dragon.

As the fire dragon manifests, you can see that his scales glow like embers of a hot fire. As his wings extend, you hear a slight sizzle and crackle. The fire dragon sways slowly from side to side, his watchful gaze upon you.

With your inner voice, greet the fire dragon with this message:

*Hail, Dragon of Fire!*
*You, who are born from flame,*
*Passionate and keen.*
*You, who slither forth from the volcano,*
*Dancing embers of heat.*
*I, [your name], greet you in peace.*

The fire dragon bows his head as an "Ah" sound joins the "M" of the earth dragon.

With a sound like the crashing of waves in an angry sea, the western quadrant of the cave begins to glow with ribbons of blue. The ribbons wave and roll for a few moments and then join to form the outline of an indigo blue water dragon.

As the water dragon manifests, you can see that her scales ripple and shine like running water. The water dragon hovers just above the cave floor as her serpentine body twists slowly. Her gaze settles upon you.

With your inner voice, greet the water dragon with this message:

*Hail, Dragon of Water!*
*You, who are born from the oceans.*
*You, who swims the rivers and streams.*

> *You, whose voice is heard in the roar of the surf.*
> *I, [your name], greet you in peace.*

The water dragon bows her head as an "E" sound joins the "M" of the earth dragon and the "Ah" of the fire dragon.

With a rush of wind, the northern quadrant of the cave begins to glow with streaks of yellow. The yellow lights rush around the cave for a few moments and begin to darken in color. When again reaching the north, the lights form into the outline of a golden dragon.

As the air dragon manifests, you can see that his golden scales are always in motion. The air dragon seems to float as his serpentine body waves slowly. His watchful gaze settles upon you.

With your inner voice, greet the air dragon with this message:

> *Hail, Dragon of Air!*
> *You, who are born from sky.*
> *You, who fly with the clouds and rain.*
> *You, whose voice is heard in the roar of thunder.*
> *I, [your name], greet you in peace.*

The air dragon bows his head as an "I" sound joins the "M" of the earth dragon, the "Ah" of the fire dragon, and the "E" of the water dragon.

Take several minutes to listen to the song of the elemental dragons as they converge.

The composition now becomes overlaid with a deep, vibrating "Om."

Above you, in the high ceiling of the cave, purple lights form. They pulse with the energy and rhythm of the dragon song. The lights join and form the outline of a deep purple spirit dragon.

With your inner voice, greet the spirit dragon with this message:

> *Hail, Spirit Dragon!*
> *You, who are born from elements.*
> *You, who are unbound in your travel.*
> *You, whose voice is heard in my heart.*
> *I, [your name], greet you in peace.*

Reach out to each of the dragons and see if they have a message for you. If they do, thank them for the message and ask what you can give in return. Listen carefully. If the dragons do request something from you, do not be shy about asking more about it, especially if it is not clear to you what it is or how to present it. Write down what you experience in your journal so you can refer to it later.

When the dragons are done with their visit, they will simply fade along with their song. When all dragons are departed or have become silent, take a deep breath and switch your focus to the back of your closed eyes.

Feel the weight of your hands. Your feet. Feel the beating of your heart.

With your next breath, you feel a shift in the energy around you. You begin to feel a bit heavier as you become more aware of your body. Slowly open your eyes when you are ready.

When you open your eyes, you will have returned to your safe space in this world. You feel refreshed by this communion with the dragons.

## JOURNAL ENTRIES

For this meditation, the following journal entries are suggested:

1. Be sure to record what the elemental dragons' message(s) were during the meditation. Were the messages delivered as a song? Spoken?

2. How did the combined elemental dragon songs make you feel? Concentrate on your senses: Did the song make you tingle inside? Can you hear the song now in your mind?

3. Compose a song or poem for the elemental dragons. When you next commune with them, present this as a gift. Write in your journal how the gift is received.

## DRAGON ENERGY
## AND ELEMENTAL DRAGONS OVERVIEW

Dragon energy is everywhere. Our entire planet pulses with energy, as do we, and to learn the technique of connecting that energy to dragons is the key to dragon magick. Be aware of the ley lines of energy that traverse our planet's surface; these "dragon lines" will aid and strengthen your connection with dragon energy. Establish a familiarity with the sacred elements and by so doing, earn the alliance of the elemental dragons.

Experience the Dragons of the Sacred Elements meditation as many times as you need until you feel comfortable with the elemental dragons. Use your journal to record any insights that may come to you.

# CHAPTER FIVE

---

# DRAGON ARCHETYPES

As you explore the dragon lore and connect with the elemental dragon spirits, you will quickly discover that there are many, many types of dragons. From the winged wyrm of Anglo-Saxon England to the serpentine Asian dragons to the fish-scaled water serpents, the dragons of legend and lore take many forms. In the spirit realm, this is also true. Along with elemental dragons, there are also archetypal dragon energies. Connecting to these archetypal dragons and their patterns of energy is a powerful channel for dragon magick.

# DRAGON ARCHETYPES

Archetypal energies in general are manifestations of a particular pattern. In order for a pattern to be formed in the spirit realm, there must be a powerful energy source and a consistent flow of energy. These patterns are constructed from energy that has purpose and focus. Songs, chants, dances, and prayers are all examples of focused energy. These spirit tools are used to connect to the spiritual realm. Likewise, patterns can also be the result of a base repetition of action, thought, or sound. Patterns formed with energetic focus are consciously connected to our world; patterns formed from repetitive but unfocused energy exist but are not aware of anything.

Dragon energy archetypes have formed over thousands of years; their patterns were shaped long ago by the telling of their tales and the rituals of their worship. The archetypes that I present here are purely from my own experiences with dragons. The commentary is my interpretation of those experiences.

In the following list, I've detailed the archetypes in alphabetical order rather than hierarchical. I also include the elemental kinships for each archetype as an aid for energetic connections. You may find additional archetypes or variations of these dragons as you progress with dragon energy.

## Ancestor Dragons

*Elemental kinship:* Spirit

*Colors:* Dark elemental colors

*Sound:* Ah

*Vibration:* Constant, slow, and methodical

Ancestor dragons are the oldest and wisest dragons. They were creators of our world; hence, their energy is connected to the roots of our world, present in every river, stream, and ocean, and in the winds. They have witnessed everything that has ever transpired; they are the keepers of memory and thought.

Their energy can feel soothing and comforting; it can also feel hard and unyielding. These dragons have no time for foolishness and will not suffer a moment of it. Yet, if they are approached with humility and sincerity, they can be moved to share their vast knowledge and wisdom.

Ancestor dragons manifest as black, gray, or bone-white dragons. Their energy has a high vibration that must be approached with care. To prepare for a connection with these spirits, read and meditate on the oldest of dragon stories. Explore the lore of Tiamat of Babylonia and Yam-Nahar of the Seven Heads from Canaan. Know that this energy is older than the earth; it expands into the cosmos and beyond what we as humans can experience or understand.

To reach out to the ancestor dragons, find a quiet, dark place where you will not be disturbed. If you cannot darken your quiet place, place a covering over your eyes and ears. Place a stone into each of your hands (any natural rock will suffice), remove your shoes (if possible), and concentrate on the energy of the earth dragons. Sense the earth dragons below the soil, slumbering quietly, and the earth dragons in the rocks—both in your hands and in the world around you. Concentrate on the connection and flow of energy between you, the rocks, the earth, and the earth dragons.

When you feel that your connection with the earth dragons is firm, turn your thoughts to what you understand as the beginning. Whatever you envision as the first moment of creation, form that visual in your mind. This might be a single point of light in a vast darkness, or a single note of music in a great silence.

At your point of beginning, reach out and connect with the stillness. Listen carefully and slow your breathing. In your mind's eye, witness the energy of the ancestor dragon as it begins to manifest. At first, you may see many dragon forms as smoky wisps of movement, then the forms will slowly spiral into a single dragon presence.

Ancestor dragons will probably demand your name and purpose before you remember to send a greeting, so brace yourself for quick but thorough scrutiny. If the dragon decides to hear your purpose, be quick and plain with your reply.

Approach ancestor dragons for a connection to knowledge and wisdom. Seek their advice for a clear path. Ask for their protection as you walk that path. Ask for their wisdom to guide you on that path.

**Some named ancestor dragons are:**

The Mushhushshu-dragon, Babylonian dragon
- The Mushhushshu-dragon is also known as the "dragon of Marduk."
- His body was covered in scales, his head was serpentine with viper horns, front feet were those of a feline with a scorpion's tale.
- *Colors:* Shades of vibrant blue and tinges of gold

Typhon, Greek dragon
- Child of the Greek gods Gaia and Tartarus
- Had a hundred dragon heads
- Volcanic eruptions are closely tied to his presence.
- His offspring includes the Hydra, the Chimera, and Ladon.
- *Colors:* Red or orange

Kur, Sumerian dragon
- Guardian of the Sumerian underworld
- His tale may be the oldest known dragon slaying lore.
- *Colors:* Black or gray

**Battle Dragons**

*Elemental kinship:* Fire

*Colors:* Colors of a flame

*Sound:* Oo

*Vibration:* Slow, fierce

When there is war in our world, battle dragons will manifest and carry that battle into realms of energy and magick. Similarly, the dragon conflicts can, and often do, determine the outcome of wars here in our world.

Battle dragons are not really concerned with the victors or the defeated; instead, they manifest primarily with the purpose of restoring balance. This is true unless the battle dragon has been purposely called to the battle or if the battle dragon has a vested interest in the outcome of the battle. Conflicts in our physical world leave horrid waste and destruction that scar and ruin the land. The creatures who dwell in the wake of war often face famine, disease, and worse. Those physical wounds echo out into the spiritual world upon waves of emotion, color, and sound.

When battle dragons detect the echoes of fighting from our realm, they will manifest at the point of conflict. These dragons will first act to minimize the infiltration of energy from our realm to theirs. What action is taken next depends on many variables, including the intensity and energetic vibration of the conflict. Battle dragons may join their energy to the conflict as an attempt to act as a tool of justice or as protectors of the innocent.

Battle dragon energy is fierce. These are dynamic dragons who have the power to dismantle both the physical and spiritual. Because you are a seeker of dragons, if you find yourself in a situation where there is a conflict, you will undoubtedly sense the presence of the battle dragons when they manifest. Their energy will feel slightly threatening and very invasive. Battle dragons manifest in the colors of battle, usually bloodred, with a vibration that feels like an explosion that never ends. Their sound is a cacophony of trumpets, drums, and war cries. When the battle dragons begin to manifest, unless you are consciously and actively participating in this conflict, it is wise to leave the area if possible. At the very least, take shelter.

If you are an activist, warrior, soldier, first responder, or the like, you will undoubtedly encounter many battle dragons. When they manifest, reach out with a part of your spirit, grasp some earth dragon energy, and hold it firmly. The earth dragon energy will ground you and aid you in attaining balance amid the powerful battle dragon energy. If the dragons actively join the conflict, then hopefully you are on the side of justice and will benefit from their interaction.

Interacting with battle dragon energy will strengthen your connections to the noble attributes of courage and fortitude. However, it is not advisable to seek or create conflict in order to commune with this energy. These dragons have a purpose that transcends any individual's needs or desires. It is possible to ally one's energy with theirs when your purpose is the same, and that is a great gift.

**Some named battle dragons are:**

Bolla, Albanian dragon

- Female dragon
- It was most likely a mature Bolla, called a *kulshedra*, that is the dragon in the tale of Saint George and the dragon.
- *Physical description:* Fiery red hair, serpentine creature
- Must remain unseen by humans in order to mature
- *Colors:* Red or orange

Dragua, Albanian dragon

- Male dragon
- True enemy of the kulshedra dragon

The Red Dragon of Britain, Welsh dragon

- The red dragon was the manifestation of the land of Britain who did battle each night with the white dragon of the Saxons.
- *Physical description:* Winged and scaled
- *Color:* Red

The White Saxon Dragon, Saxon dragon

- The white dragon was the manifestation of the armies of the Saxons as they invaded ancient Britain.
- *Physical description:* Winged and scaled
- *Color:* White

## Celestial Dragons

*Elemental kinship:* Air

*Colors:* Silver or gold

*Sound:* Om

*Vibration:* Gentle

Dragon energy flows through, into, and around the earth. So, too, does dragon energy flow throughout the cosmos. There are solar dragons, lunar dragons, and star dragons. The energy of these dragons is accessible despite the vast distances between us and them.

Celestial dragons are most often birthed from the clashing energies of cosmic creation. Their consciousness is a single part of a much larger entity, with their strongest connection being the cosmos in which they reside. Their energy contains a strong echo from the birth of the universe.

Solar dragons provide energy for the planets and other celestial bodies that revolve around them. They are mighty guardians and sustainers of life itself. They are formed from clouds of space dust, or nebulas, and are quite cold and quiet for hundreds of thousands of our earth years.[13] This energy is highly focused outward, away from itself, and has a fierce but very parental ambience. The energy from our own sun is the only way (for now) to experience this type of celestial dragon consciousness.

Solar dragons are either orange or red, depending on the age of the sun: younger suns are orange while the older suns are red. The solar dragon energy from our sun is fierce and hot, but it is approachable. You will probably first feel the pull of strong energy, but you will also feel the tension of focused movement. The movement is a reflection of and a contributor to the rhythm of the universe as a whole.

Lunar dragons are unique in that their energy is part of a symbiotic energetic relationship with another celestial (sometimes called the parent) object. For us, the earth's moon is the lunar dragon energy that we can most easily access. There is a push and pull, an ebb and tide rhythm to lunar dragon energy that is very tangible. Their energy is felt the strongest when the moon is full. You can bathe in the moonlight and feel the energy cascade and fill your physical and spiritual self. Lunar dragons manifest as a silvery-white color and have a cool, refreshing energy. Like the solar dragon energy, there is a tension here that is potent.

We met a star dragon, Ladon, and saw how a guardian dragon can be transformed into a celestial dragon. The difference between a solar dragon and a star dragon is simply its relationship to you. Star dragons have a cold,

---

13. "Stars," NASA, accessed April 5, 2023, https://science.nasa.gov/astrophysics/focus-areas/how-do-stars-form-and-evolve.

icy energy that pulses with the rhythm of the universe. Their energy comes to us across vast distances and contains glimpses into the past—not our past, but theirs. To commune with star dragon energy is to open your spiritual eyes to their path and their evolution. Star dragons are a shiny silver color; they emit and pulse with a steady, firm energy. Communing with them is the way to understand the tides of time within the infinite.

If you choose to commune with a celestial dragon, prepare yourself for the experience to be an "observe and learn" lesson. These dragons are connected to our earth and to us, but their energy is more strongly connected to being part of an infinite "whole." You will undoubtedly feel quite small and unimportant, perhaps even invisible, as you experience celestial dragon energy. Yet know that there is also strength in the humility of that observation. Knowing that you have a place and purpose in the cosmos, and endeavoring to connect to and fulfill that purpose, is sowing the dragon's teeth.

**Some named celestial dragons are:**

Draco, Greek dragon
- Transformed from guardian dragon into celestial dragon
- Guardian of the Golden Apples
- *Colors:* Silver and white

Tianlong, Chinese dragon
- Acts as a celestial guardian of heavenly palaces
- Pulls chariots for the divine
- *Colors:* Silver and white

**Deity Dragons**
*Elemental kinship:* Spirit
*Colors:* Any
*Sound:* Ah
*Vibration:* Supple

Some deities have the ability to transform into dragons and can remain in dragon form for as long as they wish. You may well meet one or more of these dragons as you walk this path, as they seem to be genuinely interested in our pursuit of wisdom and are keen to act as guides for the sincere seeker. Whether the deity's true form is that of the dragon or not is still a mystery. Know that these dragons are the keepers of honor and service.

Deity dragons manifest in many colors, shapes, and sizes. Their energy has a high vibration that is full of sound and motion. A deity dragon's energy pulses with a strong, almost booming continuous pattern of both sound and color. Like a fire dragon's energy, this flow of energy can burn, so it must be respected and approached with great awareness.

To prepare for a connection with this energy, read and meditate on the tales of the old gods and goddesses. A few of the pantheons that have direct references in their lore about their gods transforming into dragon form are the Greek, Egyptian, and Asian. There are more tales yet for you to discover; know that your energetic connection with deity dragons will be directly dependent upon your sincerity and dedication to finding those tales of transformation and meditating on them.

Deity dragons will call to you. This call may come in the form of a visual or sound, a repeated encounter with a particular symbol, or even in a dream. It is likely that you may not recognize the call at first, so use your journal diligently to record your dragon-related activities and then go back and read your entries and look for patterns.

If you feel that a deity dragon is calling to you and you are ready to connect with that energy, find a quiet place where you will not be disturbed. Make yourself comfortable and ground yourself with the energy of the earth dragons. When you feel that your connection with the earth dragons is firm, place your focus on slowing your mind. Clear your thoughts. Open your heart to the energy of the universe.

What you see, hear, and feel as you commune with a deity dragon will be your own unique experience. Deity dragons have appeared as enormous creatures with great, booming voices and startling energy. They have also appeared as tiny dragons that fit in the palm of your hand.

Since deity dragons call to you, there is no need to introduce yourself or state your purpose. They already know you well based on the efforts and energy that you have spent in pursuing knowledge of them.

Deity dragons will help you to better understand what it means to honor something greater than yourself. Their energy will help you to know what it means to give selfless and heartfelt service.

**Some named deity dragons are:**

Akhekhu, Egyptian dragon

- • Lived in the deserts and wastelands
- • *Color:* Brown and orange

Quetzalcoatl, Aztec dragon

- • God of the rain and wind
- • Feathered serpent
- • Closely tied to priestly rulership

## Guardian Dragons

*Elemental kinship:* Earth

*Colors:* Colors of nature

*Sound:* A-osh

*Vibration:* Firm

Guardian dragons are protectors of sites of worship and gateways to the spirit world.

Much of the oldest dragon lore is focused on guardian dragons, especially the Greek tales. Guardian dragons have energy that, when first encountered, feels thick and impenetrable. Depending on what or who they are guarding, these dragons range from very discerning toward anyone or anything that approaches their domain to formidable, dangerous, and most likely unforgiving.

How these dragons manifest in our world is directly influenced by their specific task as a guardian. Guardian dragons quickly reveal themselves if their domain is being threatened. They can also be called to defend an entity or place that they have agreed to defend. (This is an instance where a guardian dragon will also take on the aspects of a battle dragon.) Whatever color they may appear to embody is most likely a reflection of their surroundings. A dragon defending a vast treasure hoard might appear as a dazzling, jeweled creature. A dragon that guards a physical cave that is an entrance to another

dimension would probably have the gift of invisibility or perhaps a camouflage of mist, shadow, and silence.

Communing with guardian dragon energy is most easily accomplished
by visiting a physical location, if possible, where a guardian dragon does or
once did act as a sentinel. An example of this type of location is the Oracle
of Delphi. Delphi is a sacred site that is visited by millions each year and still
resonates with the energy of its mighty guardian, Pytho, who was slain by
Apollo ages ago.

If a physical trip is not possible, meditation within sacred space can also
allow you to experience guardian dragon energy. Ideally, find a private location, like a cave or well-hidden place, where you will not be disturbed. If you
must do this indoors, use a closet or small room. Sit in the dark with your
eyes closed and slow your breathing. In your mind's eye, visualize a mighty
dragon coiled before the entrance to a cave. Take a deep breath and reach out
to your allies, the earth dragons, and hold on to that energy.

Give your name and purpose to the guardian dragon. Do not trespass into
their domain unless you are invited to do so. From these dragons, you will
learn fealty and truth. Once you have gained their trust, they will gladly and
proudly share the tales of the mighty guardians and the knowledge that they
have gained.

Seek the guardian dragons to experience what it means to commit to a
purpose that is not born from your own need of self-preservation. Ask them
to teach you how to be a good steward in this world and beyond.

**Some named guardian dragons are:**

The Colchian Dragon, Greek dragon

- Guarded the Golden Fleece
- Key guardian aspect: This serpent never slept.
- Enormous serpent dragon

Pytho, Greek dragon

- Guarded the omphalos at the Temple of Delphi
- Enormous serpent dragon
- Slain by Apollo

## Primordial Dragons

*Elemental kinship:* Water

*Colors:* Colors of the sea

*Sound:* Eea

*Vibration:* Primal

Primordial dragon energy is created from the continual, universal cycle of chaos and creation. These dragons actively participate in this pattern as either destroyer/challenger or creator/defender.

These dragons are participants in a pattern of movement, sound, and color that is never-ending. It is a moving tapestry that contains the beginning, the end, and all that is in between. The design is ever changing: One dragon will emerge from a still point of nothingness as another dragon manifests and tears the first one into pieces. Those pieces merge into smaller dragons as another dragon forms and devours them. Just as something is created, it is destroyed, re-created, and then emerges again.

The pattern does have a consciousness, but it is so deeply contained within the vortex that it is difficult if not impossible for humans to connect with it. Their pulse is the heartbeat of the universe; the first note that ever sounded still echoes in the primordial dragon energy.

These dragons are all colors and none, every sound and profound silence, every movement and complete stillness. Their place of existence is not hindered by time or space. Their energy is perpetuity; it can be felt and experienced in meditation, but with our physical form, we cannot "touch" or attain that level of consciousness and awareness.

## Some named primordial dragons are:

Tiamat, Babylonian dragon

- Possibly the most ancient of dragons
- Fierce creator of the world
- A demanding spiritual mother figure

Yam-Nahar, Canaanite dragon

- Sea dragon
- Destructive role in chaos and creation cycle
- Power can be tamed by almost no one and nothing

## Prime Mover Dragons

*Elemental kinship:* Masters of one or more of the five sacred elements

*Colors:* Correspond with elemental kinship

*Sound:* Ah

*Vibration:* Fast and constant

Prime mover dragons are a rare manifestation of dragon energy. They are masters of at least one, or perhaps all, of the five sacred elements. Their mastery allows them to be unhindered by the limitations of our physical world and physical movement. They move seamlessly within and around our physical world by using passageways between the elements. These dragons can manifest here and then instantly "step" or "slide" into and through the elemental realms. They can then remain in the elemental realms or manifest into the physical as they choose.

Medea, from the tale of *Jason and the Argonauts*, is gifted with a pair of prime mover dragons by none other than her grandfather, the sun god, Helios. Ancient Greek vases and urns illustrate these dragons as a pair of large serpentine creatures whose coils encircle the entire chariot. These dragons appear from the sky, whisk Medea away from a life-threatening situation, and take her to safety with unusual speed.

Not unlike the deity dragons, you do not seek the company of prime mover dragons. These dragons manifest in times of great need, usually at the behest of a god, and often act as the transporters of the gods themselves.

## Some named prime mover dragons are:

Medea's dragons, Greek dragon

- Enormous and swift dragons
- Pull chariot of Helios
- Gifted to Medea

## World Dragons

*Elemental kinship:* Spirit

*Colors:* All colors

*Sound:* Aaa

*Vibration:* Balanced tension

World dragons are masters of cosmic balance. They *hold the tension* between all worlds and all things. Often called an *ouroboros*, these dragons are coiled protectively around all of creation, their tails held gently within their own mouths, holding the world in balance. This is the dragon symbol of eternity.

The world dragon is a potent symbol to use in meditation as we work toward balancing our personal lives and integrating that balance with that of the world around us. With all worlds always in motion—the microcosm and the macrocosm—achieving any kind of balance can seem overwhelming. Yet, as we have experienced with the elements, it is possible to hold the tension between ourselves and the world, between the world and the elements, even between the cosmos and all that is in it.

To work with world dragon energy, concentrate on the ouroboros symbol in your mind, or if you have a physical representation, focus your senses on it as you sit in silence. Feel the tension within the dragon's body as it remains perfectly still, its eyes wide open. Within the dragon's coils is the world—however you perceive the world during this time. From the world dragons, you will learn the value of poise and steadiness.

## Some named world dragons are:

Jormungandr, Norse dragon
- Offspring of the god Loki
- Enormous serpent that was first a sea dragon
- Harbinger of the Norse apocalyptic event of Ragnarok

Apep, Egyptian dragon
- Egyptians named him the World Encircler
- Astrologic foe of the solar deity, Ra
- Egyptian ouroboros

## MEDITATION: DRAGONS OF THE PATTERN

Take some time to reflect on and connect to the archetypal dragon energies. Add the following meditation to your dragon practice. Dragons of the Pattern is meant to connect you more strongly to the energy and mystery of the dragon archetypes.

Locate an area that is quiet and where you will not be disturbed. This can be outside or inside; the most important consideration for these meditations is that you are comfortable and feel safe. Be sure to wear clothing that does not hinder your movement and that the temperature and lighting are pleasant. Sit or lie down, whichever suits you, and close your eyes.

Breathe deeply. In and out. Concentrate on your breath as it enters your lungs, filling you with life, and then feel it exhale, leaving you energized.

Now, focus on one deep, slow breath to energize and clear your body. In and out. Another deep, slow breath to energize and clear your mind. In and out. Finally, another deep, slow breath to energize and clear your spirit.

Let the cares and concerns of the mundane world roll away from your neck… your shoulders… your arms… your fingers. Allow your back to relax, from your neck down, down, down to the base of your spine… and just breathe…

Allow your focus to rest behind your closed eyes as you feel your body relax completely. You are still. You are quiet.

In your mind's eye, see yourself on a rocky hillside. There are scatterings of dew-moistened grass. The air is clear and fresh. The sun is warm upon your face. The energy of this place, of this time, is solid, good, and strong.

You stand at the bottom slope of a tall, snow-crested mountain. As you look up, you see a path that leads up the mountain; it is a path that is becoming more familiar to you.

Begin walking upon the mountain path, slowly ascending. Each footstep is deliberate and sure. Your breathing is deep and satisfying.

Take a few more steps and you will see the familiar cave entrance in the mountain. Take a deep breath and enter the cave. Move to the center of the cavern. Concentrate on the stillness.

You hear the world dragon before you see it. There is a slight rustle of the sand and small stones of the floor as the world dragon's muscles ripple beneath its scales. The exhale of the dragon warms the room. You stand in the center of the dragon's coils, safe and protected.

Just within the coils, you now see a swirling motion of every color that you can imagine. Over and under, the energy runs along the shape of the world dragon. It darkens, sparkles, and then falls into shadow again. Deep within the coils of the dragon and the primordial energy as you stand in the center, you sense a strong, booming heartbeat. Allow your own heartbeat to join in the same rhythm.

With your inner voice, greet the world dragon with this message:

*Hail, Dragon of Eternity!*
*Beneath your scales,*
*Firm and strong.*
*Holding together the sinews of the worlds.*
*I, [your name], greet you in peace.*

The world dragon turns its eyes upon you as a ripple of energy cascades down and around its scales. A deep voice is heard in your mind.

*Hail, Seeker of Dragons.*
*I am time without end.*
*I am ever and a day.*
*I am Leviathan, ouroboros,*
*The first day and the last.*

The dragon's voice is soothing and calm. Take some time to simply be in this place, the center of the world dragon, and feel this energy.

*Take nine deep breaths.*

As you exhale on the ninth breath, you feel several other dragons manifest within the center where you are. A bone-white dragon takes a step toward you and extends its wings. It speaks with a voice that creaks from old age.

*Greetings, Young One.*
*Know me as the past.*
*I carry the treasures of knowing,*
*The thoughts and memories*
*Of those who came before.*

Take nine breaths to focus on the energy of the ancestor dragon. (Pause for nine deep breaths.)

As you exhale on the ninth breath, a red dragon emerges from the shadows. It also extends its wings as its eyes gaze into yours. Its voice is like a symphony of many.

*Behold, I am the dragon of war.*
*The dragon of blood.*
*The dragon of justice.*
*I defend.*
*I protect.*
*I respond.*
*My strength is unbounded.*
*My oath is steadfast.*
*Know me as conviction.*

Take nine breaths as you concentrate on the energy of the battle dragon. (Pause for nine deep breaths.)

As you exhale on the ninth breath, a dragon emerges that fades in and out of your sight. You realize that the dragon can perfectly camouflage with the stone walls of the cave, with the coils of the world dragon, and even with the sand and stone of the cavern floor. Its voice whispers like a soft hiss.

*Sentinel, watcher, spotter.*
*No one treads in my domain*
*Unless I wish it.*
*Shields of power.*
*Helm of Awe.*
*Sentinel, Watcher, Spotter.*

Take nine breaths as you allow the guardian dragon to study you. Do not be alarmed. Concentrate on each breath. (Pause for nine deep breaths.)

As you exhale on the ninth breath, the dragons all dissipate, and you are left alone. Take one more deep breath. You feel a shift in the energy around you. You begin to feel a bit heavier as you become more aware of your body.

Focus on the back of your eyes as you continue to breathe. Now, open your eyes. You have returned to your safe space in this world. You feel refreshed by this communion with the dragons.

## JOURNAL ENTRIES

For this meditation, the following journal entries are suggested:

1. How did it feel to be in the center of the world dragon? Describe the feel of the energy. Heavy? Light? Could you feel the tension within the coils of the dragon?

2. When the ancestor dragon manifested, what was your first thought? Do you want to commune with ancestor dragons again? What wisdom do you seek? How can you honor these ancestor dragons?

3. Battle dragon and guardian dragon energy can feel very unwelcoming, even unyielding. Were you intimidated by either or both of these dragons? What knowledge do you seek from these dragons?

## DRAGON ARCHETYPES OVERVIEW

Born and empowered from ritual and story, archetypal dragons are perpetual energy patterns. Connecting to these patterns of energy is a powerful experience. The knowledge and wisdom within these energy patterns is vast. With consistent meditation and serious study of the dragon lore of the archetypal dragons, the patterns will become more and more open. Experience the Dragons of the Pattern meditation as many times as you wish. Use your journal to record any insights that may come to you.

## CHAPTER SIX

---

# OFFERINGS
# AND SACRIFICE

In much of the dragon lore, ancient and modern, the interactions between human and dragon center around either offerings or sacrifices. These encounters are largely recalled as both violent and terrifying experiences. Typically, either human or dragon perished, and sometimes both. A destructive relationship, it seems. Unfortunately, this story motif is deeply embedded in our consciousness, both at a cultural and individual level. Yet, at the core of these encounters is the concept of great sacrifice, which is a critical component of dragon magick.

## THE SYNERGY OF SACRIFICE

Rather than dismiss these frightening tales as too disturbing—or worse, insignificant or inconsequential to modern dragon practice—we will peel back the layers of this dragon slayer story motif. In these tales there are profound mysteries at the heart of them.

Comprehending the value of sacrifice spiritually, mentally, and emotionally—and how to present such a gift—is vital to creating and maintaining a kinship with the dragons. There is sacred knowledge here in these stories, and we must find it and harvest it. First, a brief look at human sacrifice.

As distasteful as this type of offering may be, human sacrifice was indeed practiced by many cultures of the past. The Romans' practice of human sacrifice is well documented, as is the official abolishment of it in 97 BCE by the Roman Senate. In the Homeric story of Agamemnon, the gods demand human sacrifice.[14] While human and animal sacrifice were undoubtedly practiced in the past, that sort of blood sacrifice does not play a part in modern dragon practice presented in this book.

It is possible that the sacrifices in old dragon lore were part of a ritual practice. It may well be that the dragons were once worshipped. While we have no direct evidence that these sacrifices were ritual in nature, we do have cultures that, in the past and present, hold the belief that dragons are deities.

The Chinese culture, from the ancient times of the dynastic emperors to the present, deifies the dragon.[15] The focus of much of the older Chinese dragon worship was on the human form of the dragon, the emperor himself. The emperor, in turn, often prayed to the dragon for aid and advice. The people would hold cyclic dance rituals and leave offerings for the dragons in exchange for blessings. While there is no direct evidence for humans being offered specifically as part of dragon worship, the Chinese did offer humans to the gods as sacrifices.

---

14. Martinif, "Throwing Virgins into the Sea and Other Ways to Appease the Gods: The Ancient Reasons Behind Virgin Sacrifice," Ancient Origins, updated October 9, 2017, https://www.ancient-origins.net/history/throwing-virgins-sea-and-other-ways-appease-gods-ancient-reasons-behind-virgin-sacrifice-021653.

15. Leon Long, "Everything You Want to Know about Dragon Worship in China," China Educational Tours, n.d., https://www.chinaeducationaltours.com/guide/dragon-in-china.htm.

# DRAGON FOLKLORE:
## SAINT GEORGE AND THE DRAGON

Delving into the dragon lore and discovering the hidden mysteries is as much a part of a magickal dragon practice as is ritual or meditation. For example, Saint George and the dragon is a typical dragon slaying story, which involves both human and animal sacrifice. However, by shifting perspective and examining the concept of sacrifice from a magickal and ritualistic focus, a new understanding is waiting to be discovered.

Saint George is most frequently identified as the patron saint of England, but this famous dragon tale originates from the northern shores of the African continent in faraway Libya.

During George's travels, he came to the Libyan city of Silene. Here he found the people bewildered and frightened. A monstrous dragon had come out of the wild and devoured all their livestock. Adding insult to injury, the beast had then made itself at home near the city walls where it had feasted each day on two sheep, brought both as a peace offering by the villagers and intended to hold the beast at bay.

When George came along, the last of the sheep had long been sacrificed. All that the villagers had to offer were themselves. A lottery had been initiated, and each day, the dragon received two children. For the dragon to accept the offering, they both had to be under the age of fifteen.

The town was running out of children, and the king's daughter was now included in the lottery. The princess's name was inevitably drawn, and she was richly prepared for the dragon. Young and still a virgin, the people of Silene prayed that the dragon would accept the princess as a special offering and finally leave.

Upon hearing this terrifying and tragic tale, George determined that he was having none of this. He was going to rid Silene of this dragon and save the lives of the princess and those few children who remained. Hoping to challenge the dragon before it could devour the king's daughter, George armed himself and galloped on horseback to the city's walls. The dragon and

George tangled in furious combat. Eventually, George slew the dragon with his spear. George thus rid Silene of a monster.[16]

George's dragon slaying tale contains all the sacrifice motifs, human and otherwise, that were given to appease a dragon, even and especially the appearance of the sacrificial virgin. George was able to save the virgin princess in this tale, but in other similar tales, it is assumed that the dragon devours the offerings of livestock, virgins, and villagers.

How can this be anything other than a tale of fear and death? To transition your focus away from the influence of the deeply embedded dragon slayer motif, first envision the dragon as a benevolent and wise creature. Instead of wishing it to be gone, imagine that it is a great blessing for the village to have a dragon appear. There is no fear or terror of this dragon or any dragon—there is excitement and expectation. To coax the dragon to linger, offerings are made regularly. Eventually, the dragon is content, perhaps even happy with its new home. The dragon offers to share its knowledge and wisdom with a special few. For a time, the dragon and humans exist in a symbiotic relationship that is balanced and prosperous for all.

If we change to this new focus as we re-explore the lore, we can see and sense a synergy between dragon and humans. Tales of sacrifice made to dragons no longer mean the *physical* death of the offerings. From a symbolic perspective, the dragon "eating" the human is now a ritualistic action where the human is being accepted, perhaps even initiated, into a Mystery cult or religion.

## DEDICATED OFFERINGS

The dragons with which we connect today still appreciate and respond to offerings. By making offerings that come from a place of love, given with trust and a desire to evolve yourself, you will develop a more mature understanding of sacrifice. The offering is a gift; the practice of sacrificing is a commitment.

---

16. Hamilton Wright Mabie, *Heroes Every Child Should Know* (Garden City, NY: Doubleday, Page & Company, 1907), 52–55.

Thus far, we have connected with elemental and archetypal dragons and learned the technique of *holding the tension* between worlds. We have experienced the energy between the dragons, our world, and other realms. Now, it is time to strengthen your relationship with the dragons with offerings.

Offerings do not need to be expensive, glamorous, or outlandish. Simple offerings of incense or candles are just as valuable as an expensive jewel. What does matter—and it is important that you make this a practice—is that your offerings are consistent. Whether it is every morning, every Saturday, or every full moon, make this commitment and fulfill it.

Use your altar and sacred space for your dragon offerings. Use a special offering dish, incense burner, or candleholder. Again, these items do not need to be expensive; they simply need to be dedicated to this one purpose of sacrifice.

## Burnt Offerings

Burnt offerings are simple but powerful gifts for dragons. As the heat transforms the object, the smoke and aroma can be experienced by the dragons in their energy form in all realms of spirit. Candles, incense, wood, and food can be used as this form of sacrifice.

For burnt offerings of incense, you can use stick incense, cone incense, or resin and herbs on hot charcoal; these items should be available from a market or New Age store, either physical or online. The scent, herbs, or resin that you use should be based on your personal interactions with the dragons.

For the offering itself, light the incense and declare that it is dedicated to the dragons. As the heat releases the aromatic smoke, speak aloud or with your inner voice:

*Dragons of the realms,*
*I, [your name], offer the energy of this burning incense to you.*
*May this gift please you.*
*May there be peace between us.*
*May you feel welcome in this place.*

Allow the incense to burn completely and the smoke to flow without influence. When the incense has burned out, allow the censer to cool, collect the ash, and bury it in the earth.

Burning a candle is another offering that is appreciated by the dragons in the spirit realms. The type of candle does not have to be specific, but beeswax candles do burn more cleanly than oil-based candles. Scented candles can be used as well. Candle color, size, or shape does not need to be specific as an offering.

The offering is simply lighting the candle and declaring that it is dedicated to the dragons. As the wick begins to burn, speak aloud or with your inner voice:

*Dragons of the realms,*
*I, [your name], offer the energy of this burning candle to you.*
*May this gift please you.*
*May there be peace between us.*
*May you feel welcome in this place.*

If you are inclined to "dress" the candle in oils and herbs or even inscribe runes, then you are feeling a pull toward candle magick. Candle magick spells will be discussed in more detail in chapter 8.

Allow the candle to safely burn until the flame is extinguished. Collect any wax or other candle residue and dispose of it properly or use it as kindling to start a sacred fire.

Wood can also be sacrificed as a burnt offering; the warmth and energy from the fire can be soothing to the dragons in the spirit realms. Build a fire and dedicate the energy of the wood's transformation to the dragons. As an offering, the type of wood or size of the fire does not matter.

To dedicate the fire, prepare and kindle the fire as you speak aloud or with your inner voice:

*Dragons of the realms,*
*I, [your name], offer the energy of this burning wood to you.*
*May this gift please you.*
*May there be peace between us.*
*May you feel welcome in this place.*

Allow the wood to safely burn until the fire is completely extinguished. After the fire has cooled, collect the ashes and bury them in the earth.

Offering the aromas of a roasting meal to the dragons is an exceptionally nice gift. This is best done outdoors so that the aromas can freely reach the realms of spirit, but it is not impossible to make the offering from indoors. Whether you choose to prepare the meal indoors or out, make a dedication and then plan to partake of the meal yourself. Indeed, it is not the physical portions of the meal that are consumed by the dragons; the dragons absorb the energy from the transformation of the ingredients as they heat. Like us, they also enjoy the aromas of cooking food.

As you prepare the food and it begins to heat, speak aloud or with your inner voice:

*Dragons of the realms,*
*I, [your name], offer the energy of this transformation to you.*
*May this gift please you.*
*May there be peace between us.*
*May you feel welcome in this place.*

When your meal is ready, prepare yourself a plate and enjoy it. The meal becomes a shared offering for you and the dragons. Your good health and well-being are important to the symbiotic relationship that you are building with the dragons.

## Offering of Sound and Movement

Dragons love and appreciate poetry, music, and dance. Offerings of sound can be recitations of poems, singing, humming, drumming, or the playing of any instrument. Movement, whether actual dance or simple, rhythmic steps or swaying, is also a powerful gift. Composing your own words, music, or dance for the dragons is especially potent. I am not a singer or a dancer, but as a writer, I have composed poems, short stories, even entire books for my dragon allies.

If you feel awkward about sound and movement offerings, I encourage you to work through and overcome your inhibitions. Start simple with reciting a short poem for the dragons. You may be surprised at how satisfying this feels for you, and how much the dragons will appreciate both the poem and your courage.

To make the offering, go to your special place and announce to the dragons aloud or with your inner voice:

*Dragons of the realms,*
*I, [your name], offer [words, music, sound].*
*May this gift please you.*
*May there be peace between us.*
*May you feel welcome in this place.*

Establish a routine of dragon offerings and record in your journal what you offer and when. As you feel the offerings strengthen your connection to the dragons, add meditation to your dragon practice.

## ENERGY EXERCISES

Make offerings to the dragons a dedicated routine. Offerings that are sincere and from a place of trust will build a strong kinship with the dragons. The following offerings are suggested:

### Offerings of Sustenance

Food or drink offerings: Please keep in mind that food and drink left unattended may sour and attract animals and insects. Best practice for these types of offerings is to leave the items for a short period and then dispose of them properly.

- *Milk:* In my experience, milk is a dragon favorite. I use store-purchased dairy, but any type of milk will suffice. Use a dedicated drinking vessel (bowl or cup) and pour a small amount as your offering. Add a bit of sugar or honey to the milk for a special touch.
- *Water:* A vessel of clean water, perhaps blessed with a poem or song, is an excellent offering, especially for dragons who are associated with the element of water, such as the Ismenian Dragon or Jormungandr.

## Offerings of Scent and Light

Incense and candles: Offerings of incense and burning candles are simple yet effective. The energy of the incense and candle transforming as they burn is a potent gift for your dragon allies. Here are some suggested incense and candle offerings. (Indoors or out, never leave incense or a candle burning unattended!)

- *Incense resins:* Frankincense, myrrh, and dragon's blood resins all have very pleasing aromas and create gorgeous, thick clouds of smoke. (You will need a charcoal briquette and a safe place to let the resin burn.)

- *Stick or cone incense:* Frankincense, dragon's blood, myrrh, and any combination thereof along with sandalwood are excellent offerings.

- *Candles:* The candle color is more important than the type of candle; however, here are a few tips that may guide you in choosing a candle type for the offering:

  - Beeswax candles: These burn very cleanly and leave little or no candle wax to clean.

  - Petroleum-based candles (most candles): These are easy to find but burn very hot with lots of candle drippings for cleanup. They also require a proper candlestick holder. Place these types of candles on a fire-resistant surface in a candlestick holder, and do not leave unattended.

  - Homemade candles: Whether you are using a kit or know how to make candles from scratch, homemade candles are beautiful gifts for the dragons. Read a poem or sing a song as you make the candles for a special touch.

  - Candle color: Using elemental colors as the basis, here are some suggested candle colors for specific offerings:

    *Red:* Use to make an offering to the fire dragons specifically or as an offering to the dragons of love and passion.

    *Blue:* Use to make an offering to the water dragons specifically or as an offering to the dragons of peace and tranquility.

*Yellow:* Use to make an offering to the air dragons specifically or as an offering to the dragons of intellect and clear vision.

*Green:* Use to make an offering to the earth dragons specifically or as an offering to the dragons of healing and wholeness.

*Purple:* Use to make an offering to the dragons of spirit specifically or as an offering to the dragons of courage and strength.

## MEDITATION: AN OFFERING FOR THE DRAGONS

Locate an area that is quiet and where you will not be disturbed. This can be outside or inside; the most important consideration for these meditations is that you are comfortable and feel safe. Be sure to wear clothing that does not hinder your movement and that the temperature and lighting are pleasant. Sit or lie down, whichever suits you, and close your eyes.

Breathe deeply. In and out. Concentrate on your breath as it enters your lungs, filling you with life, and then feel it exhale, leaving you energized.

Now, focus on one deep, slow breath to energize and clear your body. In and out. Another deep, slow breath to energize and clear your mind. In and out. Finally, another deep, slow breath to energize and clear your spirit.

Let the cares and concerns of the mundane world roll away from your neck... your shoulders... your arms... your fingers. Allow your back to relax, from your neck down, down, down to the base of your spine... and just breathe...

Allow your focus to rest behind your closed eyes as you feel your body relax completely. You are still. You are quiet.

In your mind's eye, see yourself on a rocky hillside. There are scatterings of dry grass and brush. The air is clear and fresh. The sun is warm upon your face. The energy of this place, of this time, is solid, good, and strong.

You stand at the bottom slope of a tall, craggy mountain. As you look up, you see a path that leads up the mountain; it is a path that is familiar to you.

Begin walking upon the mountain path, slowly ascending. Each footstep is deliberate and sure. Your breathing is deep and satisfying.

Take a few more steps and you will see the familiar cave entrance in the mountain. Stand at the entrance and take a deep breath. Concentrate on the stillness.

As you stand quietly, you see shapes begin to illuminate the rock above the cave entrance. Runes appear and glow like silvery stars. You begin to hear a low hum coming from the darkness.

You notice that your hands and feet are lightly bound, not with rope but with soft cloth that smells slightly of juniper. You are dressed in a beautiful robe of linen.

You feel the earth tremble slightly. The sound of shuffled movement reaches your ears from the darkness in the cave before you. Your heart begins to race with excitement. Your breathing increases to short gasps. You hear a deep but pleasant voice speak:

*Be at peace.*
*You have nothing to fear from me.*
*Calm yourself.*
*Breathe deeply.*

Focus on your breathing. Take slow, deep breaths. When you are calm and focused again, the dragon's voice comes through the darkness:

*Have you come of your own accord?*

Answer the dragon in truth. The dragon's head emerges from the cave.

*If you have come of your own accord*
*And wish to continue, will you enter herein?*

Again, answer the dragon in truth. If you wish to enter, take a step forward.

(If you do not wish to enter, thank the dragon for this opportunity but send the message that you are not yet ready. Skip to the last two paragraphs of the meditation.)

The dragon nods its head and steps toward you. You can now see the magnificent creature's chest and forefeet.

*Come closer.*

Take three more steps toward the dragon. Focus on your breathing. The dragon seems pleased as it extends one of its claws toward you. With quick, precise movements, the dragon removes the cloth wraps from your feet and hands.

*Be welcome here.*

The dragon fully emerges from the cave and bows its head low toward you. You bow in return.

*Come, see what treasures lie within!*

The dragon stands aside and gestures for you to enter the cave. Do so with strong, firm steps. The dragon follows eagerly.

As you step into the cave, you are amazed to find yourself in the brightly lit interior of an enormous room of scrolls, books, maps, chests, and more. The strong smell of leather, wood, and paper fills your senses. The knowledge housed in this space is tangible.

*My library, says the dragon.*

As you turn toward the voice, you see that the dragon has become smaller and is lounging in front of a roaring fireplace. The dragon gestures to the room and speaks:

*The knowledge contained in my library is open to you.*
*That is, the experiences of my spirit are accessible to you.*
*I can answer your questions and will act as your guide.*
*Listen closely and hold fast what I have known.*

Take some time to explore the memory cathedral of the dragon. When you are ready (and remember, you can return here at any time), bid your new dragon ally farewell.

Take three deep breaths. You feel a shift in the energy around you. You begin to feel a bit heavier as you become more aware of your body.

Focus on the back of your eyes as you continue to breathe. Now, open your eyes. You have returned to your safe space in this world. You feel refreshed by this communion with the dragons.

## JOURNAL ENTRIES

For this meditation, the following journal entries are suggested:

1. Describe and draw the runes that appeared above the cave's entrance. Do you recognize them? Research what you saw if you do not. Is there a message? A name? Do the runes change with each meditation?

2. Describe how you felt when you realized that your hands and feet were bound. Did the bonds have a color or symbols on them? What about your robe? Describe its color and how it felt to wear it.

3. What did the dragon look like? Scaled or serpentine? Winged or not? Color? Horned? Have you seen this dragon before?

4. Record offerings that you leave for this new dragon ally, when and what, and if the offerings influence future experiences of this (or other) meditations. These offerings may take place during your meditation, or they may become part of daily interaction with the dragons.

## OFFERINGS AND SACRIFICE OVERVIEW

Understanding the value of sacrifice and how to present a proper offering to the dragons is a critical component of any dragon esoteric practice. Although the earliest dragon tales are typically dragon slayer tales, these stories do contain the keys to comprehending the mystery of ritual offering. These tales must be reexamined and re-envisioned as stories of a time when dragons and humans shared a fruitful, symbiotic relationship.

Read the old tales and make dragon offerings in a consistent and sincere manner. Make the re-imagining of the old tales a part of your dragon esoteric practice. Experience the An Offering for the Dragons meditation as many times as you wish. Use your journal to record any insights that may come to you.

# CHAPTER SEVEN

## DRAGON RITUAL

Dragon ritual is a formal act of communion with the dragon spirits. In this chapter, a thirteen-step ritual template is introduced as part of a magickal dragon practice. The ritual template is structured yet simple and is designed to awaken your spirit self and enhance your spiritual communion with dragons. The rituals in this chapter are presented as solo workings; however, they can be adapted for group ritual as well.

Like the meditations in this book, it is recommended that you use your sacred space or find a quiet, private spot for your rituals. This area can be indoors or outdoors, large or small. This is your special area for interacting with dragon energy. Make sure the space is kept clean and tidy for your rituals, and if possible, its primary purpose should be for communion with the spirit world.

## WHY RITUAL?

The philosophy behind why ritual is performed and why it works is a study that involves understanding how we as humans respond to certain stimuli in a particular setting. When our minds recognize that we are experiencing a formal time of worship or spiritual communion, our physical bodies, along with our emotional state, begin to alter. Our breathing and heart rate slow down. We begin to relax. A particular hymn or prayer may release tears of joy. A favorite poem, psalm, or surah may bring comfort and peace in its familiarity.

In the magickal tradition that I have been practicing for over twenty-five years, we teach that the purpose of ritual is for a successful communion with the spiritual world and spirit beings. We believe that words, movement, and focus are powerful tools for achieving and activating the higher spirit self. Simply put, ritual will transform your focus from the mundane, conscious world to the world of spirit and spirit beings.

When we call upon the energy of the dragons, we are awakening and bringing forth that aspect from within ourselves as well. As the energy from within us flows outward, it is united with the flow from the spirit realms where the dragons dwell. With your higher self fully awake, the spirit beings will more easily connect and communicate with you. While ritual is not necessary to interact and connect with the spirit world, a formal ritual setting will enhance and elevate your interactions with this world.

## THIRTEEN STEPS OF RITUAL

The actual steps for ritual vary depending on the esoteric tradition. My tradition uses thirteen steps. These steps are presented here with modifications for more specific references to the dragon spirits. Certainly, these steps can be used for any esoteric ritual. We believe that these components, done in order, will result in a harmonious communion with the world of spirit and those who inhabit it. By using the thirteen-step template, you are tapping into the energy of an established ritual pattern. The thirteen steps of ritual are:

1. Purpose: Establish purpose of ritual

2. Composition: Create or review existing ritual

3. Preparation: Set the stage for ritual space and self

4. Raising energy: Energize sacred space

5. Invocation: Invite the elemental dragons

6. Invocation: Invite the deity dragons

7. Petition: Request for the dragons

8. Offering: Sacrifice to the dragons

9. Thanksgiving: Gratitude for your communion with the dragons

10. Sacred feast: Blessed food and drink shared with dragons

11. Farewell: Formal goodbye to the deity dragons

12. Farewell: Formal goodbye to the elemental dragons

13. Closing the portal: Declaration that ritual has concluded

## RITUAL PURPOSE

The ritual itself begins with the clear proclamation for why the ritual is taking place. In general, communion with the spirit world tends to be more productive with an established reason for why. So, your first step for dragon ritual should be answering the question of why should you, or anyone, participate in the ritual? What will they receive, esoterically, from doing so? Why would any dragon spirits want to join your ritual space and participate in the ritual?

The purpose could be obvious. Perhaps it is a full moon and you wish to connect with and learn from lunar dragon energy. It could be a celebratory ritual for a holy day or a personal accomplishment. The purposes for ritual are going to vary. As a practitioner and seeker of dragons, it is important for you to determine the reason for each ritual and keep the ritual focused on that purpose.

When you have the reason for the ritual, declare it by stating what that purpose is. If you have a title or name for the ritual, record it in your journal. Begin meditating on the ritual and visualizing how it will be conducted.

## COMPOSITION OR REVIEW OF RITUAL

If you are going to conduct a ritual that has already been written (such as one in this book), read it closely several times and well before the planned time for the ritual. While it is not necessary to memorize the ritual, committing the words of a magickal ritual to memory is a valuable and powerful tool for activating your higher self. If you do not wish to memorize an entire ritual, you may wish to at least memorize the dragon calls for the elemental and deity dragons (provided later in this chapter).

If you are going to compose an original ritual, first, be patient and realize that the ritual will probably evolve and need to be edited multiple times. Try not to get frustrated or overwhelmed with changing your original words; ritual is a transformative process, and the ritual should (and will) reflect this. The evolution of a magickal ritual is like the polishing of a pearl: the sand can be a wee bit rough during the transformation, but the final product is beautiful.

Write a first draft, read it over, and then take some quiet, meditative time to visualize the ritual. Pay attention to what you observe in your mind's eye and note any particular colors, sounds, words, or other ritual components that stand out during your visualization. Integrate what you sense in those visualizations into the ritual. Finally, when you have sanded and polished the ritual into beautiful form, you are ready.

## RITUAL PREPARATION

Your ritual preparation began with declaring the ritual's purpose back in step one. Now that the ritual has been composed or reviewed, the time for the ritual arrives, and you should prepare in both a mundane and esoteric manner.

Your pre-ritual activities will initiate the gentle awakening of your higher self. As you gather the physical components for the ritual—candles, paper, writing device, crystals, the written ritual, and sacred feast items—your higher self is activated. Each of the rituals in this book has a list of needed items already prepared for you. It is recommended that you make a list for your own rituals; this is so that you don't have to pause mid-ritual to retrieve a forgotten charcoal briquette or bottle of oil.

For your personal preparation, a ritual bath is a lovely and effective method for awakening your higher self. The water temperature and length of the bath should be to your liking. Take the time to relax and banish any troubling thoughts from the mundane world. Focus on gently awakening your spirit self.

If you wish to add herbs or oils to your ritual bath, some common ingredients are rose petals, chamomile, rosemary, peppermint, lavender, oats, dandelion, and jasmine. Always test any herbs or oils before using them, especially if you have sensitive skin. Always include a carrier oil if using essential oils in the bath. If you have known allergies, do not use anything but clean water for your ritual bath. A ritual bath recipe can be found in appendix A.

If a ritual bath does not appeal to you, a ritual shower can be substituted. If neither of those options are desired, then spend some quiet time in a private setting prior to your communion with the dragons.

An alternative for the ritual bath or shower is a dragon's breath bath. You will need:

- Dragon's blood incense (can be purchased at most esoteric shops), cone or stick will suffice
- Censer or incense holder
- Dragon's blood oil (can be purchased at most esoteric shops)
- Carrier oil at a 2% dilution rate
- Small container for oil

Wearing loose, comfortable clothing, find a position that suits you in an area where you will not be disturbed. Light the dragon's blood incense. Hold the burning incense above your head and visualize the smoke and scent forming a doorway. Place the incense in a censer or other holder and concentrate on the rising mist. This is the dragon's breath.

Take the dragon's blood oil and carrier oil and pour a small amount into a container. Mix together and hold the container and oil above the rising dragon's breath. Dip the index finger of your right hand into the oil and then place your fingertip on your forehead. Then, place your fingertip on your heart.

Speak the words:

*I, [your name],*
*Am cleansed by the dragon's breath.*

Allow the incense to burn completely (and safely!). If you have oil left in the container, use it to anoint candles or other magickal tools if you wish.

You also need to prepare the items for your sacred feast (step 10). It is very meaningful for you and the dragons if you prepare the feast items yourself. You can craft a drink from scratch, but just using a decorative container is a nice homage to the dragons. Similarly, using a specially designated plate or platter for the food is also a respectful gesture. Preparing the food item or items in your kitchen with your own hands adds more of your energy to the sacred feast as well.

## ENERGIZE RITUAL SPACE

Your altar and ritual space are now set with the items needed for ritual, and your higher self is nearly fully awakened. It is time to begin calling energy to the sacred space. This energy will strengthen you and everything that you do in the ritual.

A good energetic kickoff is the simple lighting of a candle. Igniting a flame within a dark, quiet space acts as both a tool for seeing and as a beacon that magick is afoot. If you have incense to burn or more candles to light, visualize each action like an "on" switch for energy to flow.

Once the candles are lit and the incense is burning, further energize the ritual space with sound. The following chant will reach out beyond the sacred space and alert the dragon spirits that you have created a place for them to gather. For a dragon ritual, a variation of the traditional Witches' Rune can be used.[17]

*Eko, eko, Tiamat*
*Eko, eko, Tianlong*
*Eko, eko, Colchian*
*Eko, eko, Ismenian!*
*(Repeat Eko call 3 times.)*

*Darksome night and shining moon*
*East, then south, then west, then north*
*Hearken ye to the Dragon's Rune*
*Here we come and call ye forth!*
*Earth and water, fire and air*
*Stone and sea and sky,*
*Work ye unto our desire,*
*Hearken ye unto our word!*
*Candle and censer, trust and truth*
*Calls made to the dragon realm*
*Waken ye unto life,*
*Come ye as the charm is made*
*Dragon of stone, dragon of fire*
*Horned dragon of the sky*
*Lend your power to this space*
*And work your magick by this rite*
*By all the power of land and sea*
*By all the might of moon and sun,*
*As we do will, so it will be*
*Chant the spell and be it done!*

*Eko, Eko, Tiamat*
*Eko, Eko, Tianlong*
*Eko, Eko, Colchian*

---

17. Gerald Gardner, *The Gardnerian Book of Shadows*, 1957, Sacred Texts, https://www
.sacred-texts.com/pag/gbos/gbos36.htm.

*Eko, Eko, Ismenian!*
*(Repeat Eko call 3 times.)*

## INVOCATION TO THE ELEMENTAL DRAGONS

Once the ritual space has been energized with the Dragon's Rune, the elemental dragons are called. The elemental dragon spirits will add their energy to your ritual, and their specific elemental energy, called to each quarter, will balance the energy of the sacred space. You can use these invitations in every ritual that you perform, or you can call the elemental dragons for communion with them only.

Have candles ready to be lit for the elemental dragons that you are calling: brown or green for earth, red or orange for fire, blue or green for water, and yellow or white for air. Prepare a fifth candle as well for spirit and use a purple or dark blue candle.

To stabilize and ground the energy of your ritual space, call the earth dragons first. Face the direction where you want the earth dragon spirits to manifest, probably east or north. Hold out your hands as if in greeting and speak aloud:

*Spirits of the earth dragons,*
*Children of Mother Earth,*
*I, [your name], ask you to*
*Join me in this sacred space.*

Light the candle or candles for the earth dragons and speak aloud:

*Bring your power and protection*
*Here as I call to you now*
*With love and trust.*

Take a deep breath and allow some time for your call to be heard by the earth dragons. When you sense that the earth dragon spirits have arrived, bow your head in greeting.

Next, you will call to the fire dragons. Their fire energy will begin to merge with the earth dragon energy and create a warm, comfortable ritual space. Turn to your right 90 degrees. Hold out your hands as if in greeting and speak aloud:

> *Spirits of the fire dragons,*
> *Children of heat and flame,*
> *I, [your name], ask you to*
> *Join me in this sacred space.*

Light the candle or candles for the fire dragons and speak aloud:

> *Bring your power and protection*
> *Here as I call to you now*
> *With love and trust.*

Take a deep breath and allow some time for your call to be heard by the fire dragons. When you sense that the fire dragon spirits have arrived, bow your head in greeting.

Now, call to the water dragons. Their flowing energy will begin to merge with the earth dragons and fire dragons to further empower your ritual space. Turn to your right 90 degrees. Hold out your hands as if in greeting and speak aloud:

> *Spirits of the water dragons,*
> *Children of the sea and stream,*
> *I, [your name], ask you to*
> *Join me in this sacred space.*

Light the candle or candles for the water dragons and speak aloud:

> *Bring your power and protection*
> *Here as I call to you now*
> *With love and trust.*

Take a deep breath and allow some time for your call to be heard by the water dragons. When you sense that the water dragon spirits have arrived, bow your head in greeting.

After water, you will call to the dragons of air. Their energy will join with the other elemental dragon spirits. When they arrive, your ritual space is nearly fully energized. Turn to your right 90 degrees. Hold out your hands as if in greeting and speak aloud:

*Spirits of the air dragons,*
*Child of the wind and sky,*
*I, [your name], ask you to*
*Join me in this sacred space.*

Light the candle or candles for the air dragons and speak aloud:

*Bring your power and protection*
*Here as I call to you now*
*With love and trust.*

Take a deep breath and allow some time for your call to be heard by the air dragons. When you sense that the air dragon spirits have arrived, bow your head in greeting.

The final elemental call is to the spirit dragons. Their energy will intertwine with and then balance the earth, fire, water, and air energy. To call the spirit dragons, face the earth dragon quadrant again. Take a deep breath, then speak aloud:

*Dragons of the spirit realm,*
*Stewards of the elements,*
*I, [your name], ask you to*
*Join me in this sacred space.*

Light the candle or candles for the dragons of spirit and speak aloud:

*Bring your power and protection*
*Here as I call to you now*
*With love and trust.*

Take a deep breath and allow some time for your call to be heard by the spirit dragons. When you sense that the spirit dragons have arrived, bow your head in greeting.

## INVOCATION TO DEITY DRAGONS

Your ritual space has been energized with the Dragon's Rune, and the elemental dragons have been called. You have set a proper magickal stage, so to speak, for an invitation to the deity dragons. Deity dragons, if they choose to join you, are your honored guests. They may simply observe your rite, or they may choose to participate. The call used here is a respectful invitation to do either and acknowledge your gratitude for their presence.

Have candles ready to be lit for the deity dragons. Choose colors that are appropriate for the dragon or dragons that you are calling. For example, if your ritual is a humble invitation for any or all deity dragons to bless you with their presence, then use gold or silver candles. If you plan to honor a specific, named deity dragon, select candle colors that are associated with that particular dragon, and call each deity dragon separately with their own candle (see chapter 5, "Dragon Archetypes").

Face your altar and take three deep breaths. (If you are not using an altar, then stand in the center of your sacred space.) Light the candle or candles that you have prepared for the deity dragons. Speak aloud:

> *[Deity dragon name or gods and goddesses of the dragon realms],*
> *I humbly offer this sacred space to your presence.*
> *Guide me to know something greater than myself.*
> *Aid me to give selflessly.*
> *I, [your name], ask you to*
> *Join me in this sacred space.*

Take a deep breath and allow some time for your call to be heard by the deity dragons. When you sense that the presence of the deity dragon or dragons has entered your ritual space, bow in respect.

## PETITION

You have called to the elemental dragon spirits and invited the deity dragons to your ritual. The Dragon Rune has energized your sacred space with potent dragon energy. The time has come to declare exactly why you have created this sacred space and called the dragons here.

A formal petition should be composed and either memorized or written down. The words should clearly state the purpose for the ritual. Even when a ritual is done only for the purpose of celebration, there is an act of petition asking that your homage be accepted.

Here is an example template for a celebratory ritual:

*In this sacred space*
*Blessed and energized by the sacred dragons,*
*I come to celebrate [holiday, event, announcement, etc.].*
*This is a time of [description for ritual purpose].*
*I have created this sacred space and called to my dragon kin.*
*Let my purpose be witnessed and accepted.*

This is an example petition for a Yuletide season ritual:

*In this sacred space*
*Blessed and energized by the sacred dragons,*
*I come to celebrate the Yuletide season.*
*This is a time of joy, family, and generosity.*
*I have created this sacred space and called to my dragon kin.*
*Let this celebration be witnessed and accepted within the spirit realms.*

This is a template for a ritual where you are requesting something from the dragon spirits or you plan to work a spell or charm (more on that in chapter 9):

*I call the energy to this sacred space*
*[state specifically why you are facilitating this ritual].*
*Let this be witnessed by the dragon spirits.*
*I ask that what is witnessed be blessed.*
*So be it.*

A petition example for a ritual for the making of a charm:

*I call the energy to this sacred space,*
*My purpose is to conjure a healing charm in this magickal place.*
*Let this be witnessed by the dragon spirits.*

*I ask that what is witnessed be blessed.*
*So be it.*

If you have planned for an action to accompany the petition, this is the time for it. For example, in a Yuletide celebratory ritual, at this point you might build a sacred fire and burn a special log or seasonal object. For the making of a charm or spell, you would now begin the process of that conjuring.

## OFFERING

A dragon ritual should always include the act of giving. When you ask anything of the dragons, you should balance that request with a return offering. This is part of the synergy of a ritual offering. Truthfully, everything that you do in your ritual space is an offering to the dragons. Ultimately, we are, in effect, sacrificing a part of ourselves.

Formal ritual sacrifice can take many forms. For my dragon rituals, I offer a gift of energy created from sound and breath (sometimes referred to as a *cone of energy*), a burning candle, and a quartz crystal.

To offer the dragons a cone of energy made from sound and breath, close your eyes and calm yourself. Be sure that you are firmly grounded in your ritual space, as the vibration of the sacred space is going to quicken and move as you raise this energy. Stand before your altar or in the center of the ritual area.

Decide on a sound for your energy gift. A gentle, soothing energy can be raised with a peaceful "Om" chant. (This chant is very effective for any type of ritual.) For a heavier type of energy with an extra "kick" to it, an "Ah" sound might be more suitable. Review the dragon archetypes and meditations to find a suitable sound for your rituals.

Take a deep breath and then slowly release the air in your lungs as you quietly chant the energetic sound. Continue the sound until your breath is nearly fully exhaled, and then take another deep breath. Release the sound and breath again, and this time, the sound should be a little bit louder. Do this a third time with just a bit more intensity and volume. As you feel the energy rise and swirl around you, reach out your arms and use the holding the tension technique to keep the energy there with you.

(After your third breath is released, please note that it is not necessary to hold your breath. In fact, remember to keep breathing as you prepare to release the energy cone, or you may become light-headed or feel unsteady.)

After the third breath and sound are fully exhaled, visualize the raised energy being pulled in toward you. Hold the energy close for a few moments, (keep breathing), and then release it to the dragons with a visualization of the energy moving away from your sacred space and joining the color and sound of the dragon spirit realms.

Once the energy cone has been released to the dragons, I light a candle that I have prepared as a burnt offering for the dragons. This candle will burn until it is extinguished of its own accord. This may take several days and multiple times of extinguishing and reigniting the flame simply because you want to burn the candle safely. Do not leave a burning candle unattended! Extinguish the candle when necessary, and then light it when you can safely do so. The energy from the burning flame will flow to the dragons each and every time that it burns.

The color of the candle should be chosen per the purpose of the ritual. For example, if this is a Yuletide celebration, a green, red, or other seasonal color would be appropriate. If this is a conjuring ritual for a charm or spell, the candle color should correspond with the dragon or dragons that you have invoked to the sacred space.

To offer the candle as part of your sacrifice, ignite the flame and state that this is a gift for the dragons:

> *Let the energy and power from this burning flame*
> *Be accepted as a gift to the [ritual purpose] dragon spirits.*

Place the burning candle on your altar or in the center of the ritual space. Once your ritual is complete, be sure that the burning candle is moved to a safe place or extinguished.

My third offering to the dragons is a stone, usually a quartz crystal, that has been prepared prior to the ritual. Like the candle offering, the stone's color and type is based on the dragon spirits that have been called to the sacred space. Naturally formed crystals, quartz included, can transfer electric energy using a mechanical discharge. Quartz is used every day in technology, personal and otherwise, in such tools as our computers, watches, and other digital devices. Many esoteric practitioners use crystals to hold and transfer energy for magickal purposes.

Please note that the stone should be esoterically cleansed before the ritual. To do this, you can place the stone in cold running water, direct sunlight, or both. (There are other methods for cleansing stones, so research and find the method that works best for you.)

In the ritual space, take the cleansed crystal or stone in your left hand and hold it in front of you. Place your right hand just above the stone. Imagine a white light covering the stone. When you feel that the stone has become energetically lighter, shift it to your right hand. If you are not already, assume a standing position with your arms outstretched to either side of your body. Place your feet slightly apart. Begin to widen your stance and reach out again to the dragon spirits. When you sense the connection between you and the dragons, hold it gently but firmly. Cup the stone in your hands and bring your hands to your lips. Take a deep breath and exhale onto the stone.

As your breath touches the stone, imagine that it transforms into a swirling ball of energy. Take a second deep breath and exhale slowly onto the stone. Notice how the energy becomes thicker. Take a third deep breath and exhale again. When the ball of energy has fully formed, the energy will begin to pulse. When you sense this, gently release the ball of energy by visualizing the swirling ball moving away from your sacred space and joining the color and sound of the dragon spirit realms.

Place the physical stone on your altar or in a safe place. When the ritual is concluded, either bury the stone or place it in a body of natural water. It is not recommended that stones or crystals be used more than once as ritual offerings.

## THANKSGIVING

At this point in the ritual, it is time to prepare for closing the gateway between your ritual space and the dragon spirit world. You have created a powerful portal that has allowed the world of the dragon spirits and our world, the physical world, to coexist and mingle. It would be irresponsible and disrespectful to leave that magickal portal open and unattended.

The closure of the portal begins with gratitude to the dragon or dragons for joining their energy to yours. In my experience, gratitude, in its most simple form, is more than enough for the dragons. However, not expressing your appreciation at all, or doing so poorly, will not be well received and may harm your relationship with your dragon allies.

Simply speak your gratitude, and then bow your head in a respectful manner. Here is an example of thanksgiving to the dragons:

> *Dragons who have graced this magickal space,*
> *I thank you for the gift of your love, power, and protection.*
> *Linger if you wish.*
> *Depart if you must.*
> *Let there always be peace between us.*

## SACRED FEAST

Spiritual communion with the dragons is a wonderful experience; it should feel familiar, comforting, and empowering. However, without years of ritual experience and special preparation, our physical bodies do not respond well to being in this energetic state for long periods of time. Therefore, an important step of ritual is to share a sacred feast with the dragon spirits who have chosen to join you. As discussed in chapter 6, although the dragon spirits will not actually partake of the physical food and drink, they will enjoy other sensory aspects of the feast.

Another reason why the sacred feast step of the ritual is so important is your body's physical reaction to the partaking of the food and drink. As your body reacts to the food and begins the digestive process, your higher self begins to quiet. Naturally, your focus turns to the sensory effects of what your body is experiencing. Be cautioned, without a proper grounding after ritual, you may experience dizziness or nausea.

Many esoteric traditions use a simple wine libation and a specially prepared cake or bread. The food and drink used is typically supportive of the ritual purpose. For example, a Yuletide celebratory ritual might have a rich, red wine or sweet apple cider as the drink with a sweet gingerbread cake as the food.

You can certainly enrich your sacred feast. If you want to prepare a proper plate of food that is freshly cooked, then add that to your ritual preparation list. Choose a drink that compliments the meal and include bread and dessert. Take your time and enjoy the meal in your ritual space. Know that the dragons are pleased with this type of communion with their human companions.

## FAREWELL TO DEITY DRAGONS

The dragons who have chosen to join your ritual space may remain as long as they wish (and you should not be surprised if they do linger), but it is appropriate to bid them a proper farewell nonetheless.

Face your altar and take three deep breaths. (If you are not using an altar, then stand in the center of your sacred space.) Speak aloud:

> *[Deity dragon name or gods and goddesses of the dragon realms],*
> *Thank you for joining this ritual.*
> *Thank you for witnessing that which was done.*
> *Always remind me that there is something greater than myself.*
> *Aid me to give selflessly.*
> *I, [your name], thank you.*

Take a deep breath and allow some time for your call to be heard by the deity dragons. When you sense your words have been acknowledged, bow in respect.

## FAREWELL TO ELEMENTAL DRAGONS

The elemental dragons may also linger in your space, but like with the deity dragons, it is appropriate to bid these dragon spirits a proper goodbye.

Start again in the earth quadrant of your sacred space (probably east or north), and then move clockwise around the space until you again reach the earth element. Speak these words at each elemental quadrant:

> *Dragons of [corresponding element],*
> *Thank you for this communion.*
> *Thank you for the gift of your energy.*
> *I am humbled by your presence.*

*I am grateful for your wisdom.*
*It is done.*

## CLOSING THE PORTAL

Your ritual will be complete once you declare that the sacred space is open and the portal between the worlds has been closed. Open the space by extinguishing the deity dragon candles and the elemental dragon candles.

Go to your altar and extinguish the deity dragon candle or candles. Walk to each elemental quadrant, beginning with earth, and extinguish those flames as well. When the last candle flame has been put out, speak these words:

*This rite has ended.*
*This portal between worlds is now closed.*
*So be it.*

Visualize the space returning to a completely physical environment. Take three deep breaths and concentrate on the present. When you are ready, open your eyes and prepare to celebrate. Your ritual is done!

What follows here are two dragon rituals that you can incorporate into your own dragon practice or edit as you deem fit. These rituals have been performed solo and with my magickal group. Please note that I do not include all thirteen steps for each ritual. Take the parts included here and transfer them as needed to your own ritual template wherever you deem appropriate.

## RITUAL: THE SINGING DRAGON RITUAL

There are dragons who love music, whether they are the audience or the performer. This ritual is designed to facilitate a setting where you invite dragon energy to your sacred space for the sole purpose of making music and song.

Before you begin this or any ritual, be sure that you are calm and have banished the mundane cares of the world from your mind. Make yourself comfortable. Once you are relaxed and free from worry, enter the ritual space.

**Preparation:** Three white candles, candleholders for all candles, DragonSong incense (recipe in appendix A), a heatproof container with 2–3 charcoal briquettes, lighter or matches, and a small tissue bag of DragonSong incense. Have any musical instruments or music items in the sacred space as well. Light the charcoal briquettes 10 minutes before you begin the ritual.

**Invocation:** Stand with your arms outstretched and speak these words:

> *Hail to the dragon singers!*
> *Welcome to the dragon dancers!*
> *I bid you welcome to this space!*
> *Hail to you, DragonSong!*

**Petition:** Light the candles and sprinkle incense onto the charcoal. Prepare to perform the first (or only) song or poem. Hold any instruments or other items for the performance in your hands. Speak these words:

> *DragonSong!*
> *I ask that you bless these objects*
> *With your joy,*
> *With your love.*
> *So that they, in turn,*
> *May bring joy and happiness*
> *To those who may hear my words.*

Play the songs, recite the poems, and listen for the dragons to join you in your celebration. This ritual is a celebration of music, so by all means, have fun and enjoy.

When the songs and music are done, make your offering.

**Offering:** Take the small tissue bag of DragonSong incense and hold it in your hands. Speak these words:

> *May you be pleased with this offering*
> *Given in love and trust.*

Place the tissue bag of incense onto the charcoal briquettes and allow it to burn.

**Thanksgiving:** Speak your gratitude:

> *Spirit of the singing dragon,*
> *Thank you for this communion.*
> *Thank you for the gift of your energy.*
> *I am humbled by your presence.*
> *I am grateful for your wisdom.*
> *It is done.*

If possible, allow the candles to burn completely and then safely dispose of the remains for both the candles and incense.

## RITUAL: THE SHADOW DRAGON RITUAL

There are dragons that we seek but can never seem to find. They are always on the peripheral of our senses, just beyond our ability to make an energetic connection.

These are Shadow Dragons. They do not interact directly with humans, but they are here, and they do have a purpose. If you wish to attempt an energetic communion with these dragons, this ritual is designed to open a doorway for just that.

Before you begin this or any ritual, be sure that you are calm and have banished the mundane cares of the world from your mind. Make yourself comfortable. Once you are relaxed and free from worry, enter the ritual space.

**Preparation:** Black or gray candles, candleholders, Elder Dragon incense (recipe in appendix A), a heatproof container with 2–3 charcoal briquettes, lighter or matches, and three smoky quartz crystals. Light the charcoal briquettes 10 minutes before you begin the ritual.

**Invocation:** Stand with your arms outstretched and speak these words:

*Hail to the Shadow Dragons.*
*Hail to the darkness,*
*Friend of the black night,*
*Child of the cosmos.*
*Hail to you, Shadow Dragon!*

**Petition:** Light the candles and sprinkle incense onto the charcoal. Take the three smoky quartz crystals into your hands and hold them outward. Speak these words:

*Shadow Dragon,*
*I offer you these earth stones.*
*May you infuse them*
*With your blessings*
*So that they, in turn,*
*May bring communion*
*Between you and I,*
*Between worlds.*
*It is done.*

Place the three crystals where they will not be disturbed for now. When the ritual is concluded, use these crystals in meditations, moon rituals, or energy workings to continue building a relationship with this dragon energy.

**Offering:** Take a small amount of the Elder Dragon incense and hold it in your hands. Speak these words:

*May you be pleased with this offering*
*Given in love and trust.*

Place more incense onto the charcoal briquettes and allow it to burn.

**Thanksgiving:** Speak your gratitude:

*Dragons of Shadow,*
*Thank you for this communion.*
*Thank you for the gift of your energy.*

*I am humbled by your presence.*
*I am grateful for your wisdom.*
*It is done.*

If possible, allow the candles to burn completely and then safely dispose of the remains for both the candles and incense.

## RITUAL EXERCISES

Ritual can be a powerful and transformative experience that strengthens our connection to the dragons. What's more, ritual acts as a tool, just like a candle or crystal, to empower and enhance the energy exchange with the dragons.

There are rituals, chants, dragon calls, and recipes for incenses and oils in this book, and using them will enhance your transformation as you sow the dragon's teeth. However, composing your own rituals and ritual elements can lead to an even deeper understanding of "why ritual"?

### Ritual Composition

Use one of the rituals in this book as a template and compose a ritual of your own design. Remember to first determine the purpose of the ritual. Meditate on the ritual and record in your journal what you want to achieve. Here are some suggestions for composing the ritual:

- Determine whether you want this ritual to be a day ritual or an evening ritual and why.
- Will this be a silent ritual, or will you speak, sing, or chant to the dragons?
- What will be your offering to the dragons? Consider something that you made, such as a song or poem.
- Take the time to read through your ritual and visualize it during a meditation. Make any changes that come to you.
- Perform the ritual. Remember to record the experience in your journal.

### Incense and Oil Creation

Making your own incense and oils, or perhaps even candles, will certainly enhance your dragon rituals. Here are a few suggestions for these activities:

• *Incense:* First determine whether you want to make stick incense or incense to burn in a censer. If stick incense, there are kits that can be purchased at herb and Neopagan shops, online and in the real world, that make this process quite simple. For incense that you plan to burn on charcoal or coals, you will need a mortar and pestle to prepare and combine it. You can get your resins or herbs at a shop along with the mortar and pestle.

  – Mortar and pestle: For dragon magick practitioners who make their own incense recipes, the mortar and pestle will become another magickal tool. Select one made from natural stone, if possible, and use it only for dragon-related activities.

  – Resins: Incense burns more readily and is longer lasting in its burn with resins as a key element. For dragon work, frankincense, myrrh, and amber are fantastic resins to use.

  – Dried herbs: These ingredients usually burn quite quickly and should be considered flavorful ingredients to an overall aromatic presentation.

  – Practice: While some people have a talent for making incense, others such as myself must practice, practice, practice. You will learn which resins work more effectively with the herbs as you try varying combinations. Beyond that, be prepared to make some mistakes, perhaps even dreadful-smelling concoctions. Learn to laugh at those errors, note them, and move onward.

  – Research: Please research any and all herbs that you want to include in a recipe.

• *Oils:* You should determine whether you want to purchase all of the oils that you want to use in the recipe or if you want to try making the oils yourself. If you plan to purchase the oils and combine them, then any herb or Neopagan shop should have a wide variety available for you.

  – Purchased oils: Oils should be in a dark glass container when purchased since light will affect the oil's longevity, aroma, and potency.

- Homemade oils: Oils made by the practitioner will require a metal saucepan and some form of heat; either stovetop or fire coals will work. (Once used for making oils, the pan should not be used for preparing food.) Use a non- or lightly aromatic oil as your base oil, such as sunflower oil. Using the lowest heat setting or position, gently warm the base oil until you see smoke beginning to form above the oil. Add your resin or herb in small amounts until you begin to smell the aroma of the ingredient. Remove the pan from the heat and pour the oil and herbs into a dark glass container and seal it. Later, after the oil has cooled, add just a tiny bit of clean water to the container of oil.

- Practice: As with the incense recipes, you may need to practice, fail, and try again before you become adept at making and combining oils. Through perseverance and time, you will learn which oils combine more successfully with others. If you are cooking your own oils, with experience, you will know when to add your magickal ingredients. As always, expect to make some errors that result in unusable oils. Simply learn to note what did not work and keep trying.

- Research: Please research any and all oils that you want to include in a recipe.

## DRAGON RITUAL OVERVIEW

Understanding why and how we perform ritual is crucial to a successful spiritual awakening—a transformation—through dragon energy. In this chapter, ritual was presented and explained as a powerful conduit for communing with dragon energy. Ritual should and will transform your focus from the ordinary world to the world of the dragons. In the space of ritual, you will find that communing with the dragons is easier and faster. The dragons will also find you more easily within the sacred space where a ritual is being performed. Again, ritual is not necessary to interact and connect with spirit dragons; however, it does create a potent yet still simple energetic setting that will enhance and elevate your interactions with dragons.

Rituals can certainly be more elaborate and include other components such as chanting, singing, or dancing. As your relationship with the dragons progresses, you will likely add details to your rituals that are personal to your own dragon practice. Likewise, the words that you speak to the dragons may change as your communion continues.

## CHAPTER EIGHT

# LUNAR DRAGON MAGICK
# AND RITUAL

The energetic current between the earth and the moon is a potent form of magick. The energy exchange between us and the moon is formed from our intuitive and physiological reactions to the position of the moon in relation to earth. Simply put, the gravitational pull of the moon is a powerful influence on our physical bodies and our higher spiritual selves.

The flavor of lunar dragon ritual and magick presented in this chapter observes and connects with both the new moon and full moon phases of the moon's cycle. This includes a ritual template for a new moon and a ritual template for a full moon, wherein the rituals are connected in purpose. Specifically, the new moon ritual focuses on the petition, and the full moon ritual concludes the working with acknowledgment and thanksgiving. The time in between the new moon and full moon is the manifestation phase for the petition.

## CONNECTING WITH THE MOON DRAGON

The lunar dragon energy discussed in this chapter, which is so influential in our lives, is simply called moon dragon. She has many faces that coincide with the lunar phases. She is always in motion, tugging and resisting with the waters of the earth, and her silver light fills the sky with energetic potential when she is full. Learning to work with this lunar dragon energy and harnessing it to transform ourselves and our world is the goal of this chapter.

The purpose for the new moon ritual is to connect with moon dragon energy and present a request. The request could be for special blessings for yourself or a loved one, assistance to find new employment, dragon blessings for a magickal charm, or simply to enjoy the gift of energetic communion with the dragons. Whatever your reason for this ritual is, make sure it is clear and focused in your mind before you begin composing.

You will use the thirteen-step template introduced in chapter 7 with specific lunar energy accommodations for the new moon phase. Celestial rituals are best experienced outdoors in a location where the night sky is clearly visible. However, if inclement weather or other conditions necessitate an indoor ritual, using creative visualization will suffice. For the new moon, select an evening when the waxing crescent moon is visible in the sky.

## TOOLS FOR LUNAR RITUALS

The magickal tools used in these lunar rituals are candles and crystals. The candle is used to invite the lunar dragon spirits to the sacred space and act as a beacon for them to join the ritual. There are designated candle colors for each dragon moon included below, but a white candle is always an option as well. The reason for this is simple logistics: if no colored candle is available, the white candle can be substituted.

Along with the candle, have a candleholder, as you will need to let the candle burn completely. It is perfectly fine if the candle needs more time to burn after your ritual is complete. Extinguish the flame (do not leave a candle unattended!), and relight it when it is convenient. Simply allow it to safely burn before the next ritual. Of course, matches or a lighter will also be necessary.

To aid with the energy offerings, the rituals use quartz crystals. Please note that each ritual also has the option of using a clear quartz crystal. Like the white candle option, the reason for this is simple logistics: if no colored quartz is available, the clear quartz can be substituted.

Remember from chapter 7, when you receive your crystals, you will want to energetically cleanse them before using them in ritual. (You don't know who has been handling the crystal before it arrived!) Cleansing is simple and necessary: Run cold water over the crystals or place them in direct sunlight. Keep the crystals in a quiet, dark place until it is time for ritual.

## A BRIEF REVIEW OF RITUAL

Over time, you will compile a collection of written rituals that you can reuse and refurbish as your ritual practice evolves. However, to gain this archive of rituals, you must compose the first one.

While it is true that some ritual practitioners use very lofty language in their rituals—even implementing a rather jarring mix of poor Early Modern English smashed with modern lingo—none of that is necessary. The language of your rituals, your word choice and cadence, should be simple and honest. If you are a poet, you may find that your rituals have a definitive rhythm and rhyme. If you are a vocalist, you may find that singing your rituals is your preferred flavor of magick.

Use words that clearly convey your ritual in all aspects. Compose the first draft and read it aloud. Engaging your sense of hearing will aid you in tidying up the writing process. Try to allow yourself a few weeks to read and edit the ritual.

Rituals can be as elaborate as you wish or as simple as you in sacred space with a few candles and burning incense. Remember, rituals evolve just as we do, so expect your rituals to change as you continue your magickal dragon practice.

As in chapter 7, it is worth stating again that while it is not necessary to memorize any part of a ritual, committing the words of a magickal ritual to memory is a valuable and powerful tool for activating your higher self. Consider memorizing parts of your rituals or the invocations.

## NEW MOON RITUAL PREPARATION

The purpose of this new moon lunar ritual is to connect with the moon dragon energy and present a request. You will use the thirteen-step template introduced in chapter 7. For this ritual, select an evening around the new moon.

### Ritual Preparation

Prepare your altar, sacred space, and yourself for the ritual as previously described. Clean the altar and place your ritual items and tools where you can easily reach them. You will need elemental dragon candles, a lunar candle (any color), paper and writing utensil, firesafe bowl, and food for the sacred feast. Take a ritual bath or shower (or dragon's breath bath as described in chapter 7). Wear comfortable clothes that do not inhibit your movement.

### Energize and Invoke

First chant the Dragon's Rune to charge your sacred space. Then invite the elemental dragons to your sacred space. Both are outlined in chapter 7.

### Invocation to the New Moon Dragon

The invitation for the new moon dragon is a variation of the deity dragon invocation used in chapter 7. Take the candle that you have prepared for this ritual and hold it in your left hand. Tip the candle's wick toward the ground. With your right hand, slowly sweep down the length of the candle as you visualize the candle beginning to slightly glow. Hold the candle aloft, point it toward the crescent moon, and visualize the candle's glow becoming brighter.

Light the candle and speak these words aloud or in your mind:

*Moon Dragon, I, [your name],*
*seek to commune with you.*
*I light this candle as a beacon for you.*
*Let the flame from this candle provide the energy*
*For us to meet and commune tonight*
*Here in this sacred place,*
*Here under the new moon of [month, season, or specific lunar moon name].*

Place the candle where it can safely burn during the remainder of the ritual.

## Petition

Place your focus on the shape, light, and shadow of the new moon. With your inner voice, speak these words:

*Moon Dragon, I, [your name],*
*seek to commune with you tonight.*

Take a comfortable position sitting or standing, with your hands before you and palms open. Turn your face toward the crescent moon. Clear your mind and focus again on the moon's shape, light, and shadow. Keep your eyes open but allow your gaze to soften. Now, slowly close your eyes until your vision begins to blur slightly. Hold that space. With your inner spirit, reach out even further toward the moon. Feel the tension between the gentle pull of the new moon and the strong grounding energy of the earth.

Imagine a white dragon with silver-tipped scales. She is gazing at you curiously from the crescent moon. The energy between you and the dragon grows stronger and begins to glow with soft, white light. The dragon's mind speaks to yours:

*What is it that you desire?*

Respond with your petition:

*I, [your name],*
*Ask for the knowledge, strength, and wisdom*
*To [ritual purpose].*

*I ask for my spirit to join with yours, here and now.*
*I ask that during this lunar cycle,*
*You will guide me in how to fulfill this goal.*

A simple yet effective type of petitionary magick is to write the request. Take a plain piece of paper and writing utensil and write more details about your petition: For whom is it? For how long is this energy needed? Is there a specific location where you need the energy to manifest? Compose your petition so that your purpose is stated plainly and to the point; consider this a formal written request, if you will, for the dragons.

When the petition is complete, fold or roll the paper so that the written words are fully covered. Hold the paper in your hands and concentrate on the energy of your written words. See the words on the paper as they begin to glow. Imagine the energy between you and the moon dragon growing stronger. A stream of energy begins to flow between you. This is the moon dragon current.

Now, release the energy of the petition into that current. Light the paper with the flame of the ritual candle and place the written petition into a fire-safe bowl. Let the petition burn completely. Take any ash that is left and bury it later where it will not be disturbed. (Please do not release any ash to the winds! There might still be an active spark that you cannot see!)

## Offering

Your sacrifice for the new moon working will be a simple raising and giving of energy to the lunar dragon. If you are not already, assume a standing position. Stretch your arms outward and to either side of your body. Place your feet slightly apart. Begin to widen your stance and reach out again to the current of energy between you and the dragon. As you feel the tension between you and the dragon begin to tighten, take several deep breaths. Relax your muscles. Hold onto that tension gently but firmly. Take another deep breath, and as you exhale, begin a quiet vocalization of the sound "Om." As the breath leaves your body, envision it entwining with the "Om" sound.

Your expelled breath begins to vibrate gently. Hold that energy for a moment and imagine that it transforms into a silvery liquid substance. Let the "Om" sound fade. Take a second deep breath, and with this exhale, begin another quiet vocalization of the sound "Om." As the breath leaves your body, envision the breath entwining with the "Om" sound. Your expelled breath begins to vibrate as it joins with the first silvery breath. Hold the energy of those two breaths as they continue to grow in strength. Let the "Om" sound fade. Take a third deep breath and release another quiet vocalization of the sound "Om." As the breath leaves your body, continue to envision the breath entwining with the "Om" sound. Your expelled breath begins to vibrate as it joins with the silvery energy still pulsing before you. Let the "Om" sound fade. Now, very gently, nudge the pulsing silver energy ball toward the moon dragon current. When the energy ball nears the current, it will quickly immerse itself into the flow. Allow this to happen and simply observe.

## Thanksgiving

Take a comfortable position and relax. Allow yourself to again feel the strong pull of the earth below you. Breathe gently and normally. Feel the goodness and the beauty of the world around you: the sky, the planets, all celestial objects. Feel the space in between these things. Speak your gratitude:

> Moon Dragon, I thank you for this communion
> and especially for the gift of your energy.
> My energy is now joined to yours
> for the purpose of granting the means to [ritual purpose].
> During this lunar cycle,
> I will listen and be mindful of your guidance
> So that I may fulfill this goal.
> It is done.

## Sacred Feast

Now, the time has come to share the sacred feast with the dragon spirits who have chosen to join you, and to begin grounding yourself as you prepare to end the ritual.

You can use a cup of wine and a special type of cake or bread, or you can prepare a freshly cooked plate of food. Select a drink that you like and remember to take your time and enjoy the meal in your ritual space. As you partake of the sacred feast, your higher self begins to quiet, and your physical self becomes stronger.

## Farewell to Lunar Dragon

Face your altar and take three deep breaths. (If you are not using an altar, then stand in the center of your sacred space.) Speak aloud:

> *Moon Dragon,*
> *Thank you for joining this ritual.*
> *Thank you for witnessing that which was done.*
> *Linger if you wish.*
> *Depart if you must.*
> *Let there always be peace between us.*
> *I, [your name], thank you.*

When you are finished speaking, bow respectfully.

## Farewell to the Elemental Dragons

The elemental dragons may choose to extend their visit to your space, but you should bid these dragon spirits a proper goodbye.

Start again in the earth quadrant of your sacred space (probably east or north), and then move clockwise around the space until you again reach the earth element. Speak these words at each elemental quadrant:

> *Dragons of [corresponding element],*
> *Thank you for this communion.*
> *Linger if you wish.*
> *Depart if you must.*
> *Let there always be peace between us.*
> *It is done.*

When you are finished speaking, bow respectfully.

### Closing the Portal

Go to your altar and extinguish the lunar dragon candle or candles. Walk to each elemental quadrant, beginning with earth, and extinguish those flames as well. When the last candle flame has been put out, speak these words:

> *This rite has ended.*
> *This portal between worlds is now closed.*
> *So be it.*

Visualize the space returning to a completely physical environment. Take three deep breaths and concentrate on the present. When you are ready, open your eyes. It is done.

## BETWEEN THE MOONS

The time between a new moon working and the approaching full moon is the manifestation phase. As the energy of the moon increases with its visibility in the night sky, so, too, will the energy of the moon dragon current. While the moon is full, the energy will be at its peak.

During the manifestation phase, back here in the mundane world, be mindful of clues for how to help manifest what you have requested. For instance, knowledge for how to better protect your loved ones might come in the form of an unsolicited news article about a recent increase in crime that you discovered during a (seemingly random) internet search. You might run into a friend who has a home security system that is exactly what your elderly mother could manage on her own. The point is that the knowledge and means to help fulfill your petition will come to you in a variety of ways. Together, your physical self, your spirit self, and the moon dragon energy will all work to manifest your petition. It will indeed take time, patience, and diligent observation to learn the language of how spirit transmutes into the physical world.

When the moon is full, you are ready to complete the working with the energy of the full moon.

## FULL MOON DRAGON RITUAL

The purpose of this full moon lunar ritual is to connect with the moon dragon energy and complete the manifestation of your request from the new moon petition. You will again use the thirteen-step template introduced in chapter 7 for the full moon ritual. For this ritual, select an evening when the full moon is visible in the sky.

Since this is a continuation of the new moon magickal working, use the new moon ritual and make edits for the full moon aspects. Write the ritual down or type it and print it.

### Ritual Preparation

Prepare your altar, sacred space, and yourself for the ritual. Clean the altar and place your ritual items and tools where you can easily reach them. You will need elemental dragon candles, a lunar dragon candle (any color), a clear quartz crystal, and food for the sacred feast. Take a ritual bath or shower (or dragon's blood bath as described in chapter 7). Wear comfortable clothes that do not inhibit your movement.

### Energize and Invoke

Chant the Dragon's Rune to charge your sacred space. Invite the elemental dragons to your sacred space. Both are outlined in chapter 7.

### Invocation to the Full Moon Dragon

The invitation for the full moon dragon is a variation of the deity dragon invocation used in chapter 7 and appendix A. Take the candle that you have prepared for this ritual and hold it in your left hand. Tip the candle's wick toward the ground. With your right hand, slowly sweep down the length of the candle as you visualize the candle beginning to slightly glow. Hold the candle aloft, point it toward the full moon, and visualize the candle's glow becoming brighter.

Light the candle and speak these words aloud or in your mind:

*Moon Dragon, I, [your name],*
*Seek to commune with you.*

*I light this candle as a beacon for you.*
*Let the flame from this candle provide the energy*
*For us to meet and commune tonight*
*Here in this sacred place,*
*Here under the full moon of [month, season, or specific lunar moon name].*

Place the candle where it can safely burn during the remainder of the ritual.

## Petition

Focus on the round shape and the silvery light of the moon. Watch as the light shimmers and dances into the shape of a giant white dragon with silver scales. With your inner voice, speak these words:

*Moon Dragon, I, [your name],*
*Seek to commune with you tonight.*

Take a comfortable position sitting or standing, with your hands before you and open. Turn your face toward the full moon. Clear your mind and focus on the dragon. Keep your eyes open but allow your gaze to soften. Now, slowly close your eyes until your vision begins to blur slightly. Hold that space. With your inner spirit, reach out toward the moon. Feel the enormous tension between the strong pull of the full moon and the equally strong energy of the earth.

Know that the dragon's attention is fully on you. The energy current between you and the dragon is tangibly strong and glows brightly with a pulsing white light. The new moon dragon has become full moon dragon. You were a crucial element of her transformation; your energetic gift at the new moon was an aid to the rebirth of the full moon.

The dragon's mind speaks to yours:

*State your purpose.*

Respond with tonight's petition:

*I, [your name],*
*Ask for the energy shared between us at the new moon*

*To manifest tonight here in the mundane world.*
*I ask that together we may bring this task to fruition.*

## Offering

The offering for the full moon working will be the gift of a clear quartz crystal. Place the crystal in your left hand and hold it in front of you. Place your right hand just above the tip of the crystal. Imagine a white light covering the crystal and cleansing away any energetic impurities. When you feel the crystal become energetically lighter, place it in your right hand.

If you are not already, assume a standing position with your arms outstretched to either side of your body. Place your feet slightly apart. Begin to widen your stance and reach out again to the dragon energy current. When you sense the tension between you and the dragon, hold it gently but firmly. Cup the crystal in your hands and then bring your hands to your lips. Take a deep breath and exhale onto the crystal. As your breath touches the crystal, imagine that it transforms into a silvery cloak. Take a second deep breath and exhale slowly onto the crystal. Notice how the silvery cloak of energy becomes thicker. Take a third deep breath and exhale again on the crystal. When the cloak of silver has fully enveloped the crystal, the energy will begin to pulse. When this happens, gently release the energy by visualizing the crystal floating from your hands and entering the dragon current. Observe and wait for the current to deliver the silver energy to the full moon dragon.

Take the crystal and place it upon the altar for now. After the ritual is complete, you can bury the stone in the earth.

## Thanksgiving

Take a comfortable position and relax. Allow yourself to again feel the strong pull of the earth below you. Breathe gently and normally. Speak your gratitude:

*Moon Dragon, I thank you for this communion.*
*My energy and yours have joined with purpose.*
*I am mindful of your guidance for this manifestation.*
*I am but a humble seeker.*
*It is done.*

### Sacred Feast

Gather your sacred feast items and enjoy the food and drink. Remember to take your time and appreciate the meal in your ritual space. As you eat and drink, your higher self begins to quiet as your physical self becomes stronger.

### Farewell to Full Moon Dragon

Face your altar and take three deep breaths. (If you are not using an altar, then stand in the center of your sacred space.) Speak aloud:

> *Moon Dragon,*
> *Thank you for joining this ritual.*
> *Thank you for witnessing that which was done.*
> *Linger if you wish.*
> *Depart if you must.*
> *Let there always be peace between us.*
> *I, [your name], thank you.*

When you are finished speaking, bow respectfully.

### Farewell to the Elemental Dragons

The elemental dragons may choose to extend their visit to your space, but you should bid these dragon spirits a proper goodbye.

Start again in the earth quadrant of your sacred space (probably east or north), and then move clockwise around the space until you again reach the earth element. Speak these words at each elemental quadrant:

> *Dragons of [corresponding element],*
> *Thank you for this communion.*
> *Linger if you wish.*
> *Depart if you must.*
> *Let there always be peace between us.*
> *It is done.*

When you are finished speaking, bow respectfully.

## Closing the Portal

Go to your altar and extinguish the lunar dragon candle or candles. Walk to each elemental quadrant, beginning with earth, and extinguish those flames as well. When the last candle flame has been put out, speak these words:

*This rite has ended.*
*This portal between worlds is now closed.*
*So be it.*

Visualize the space returning to a completely physical environment. Take three deep breaths and concentrate on the present. When you are ready, open your eyes. It is done.

# DRAGON MOONS

You may wish to observe and connect with the lunar dragon energy for each phase of the moon. For each lunar cycle of the calendar year, here are the names of the dragon moons that I use and their crystal, candle, and energy focus correspondences.

## First Winter Lunar Cycle

- *New moon:* Sky Dragon Moon
- *Full moon:* Snow Dragon Moon
- *Crystal:* Clear quartz
- *Ritual candles:* Silver and white
- *Energy focus:* Protection for loved ones. Petition for security and protection from harm.

## Second Winter Lunar Cycle

- *New moon:* Sky Dragon Moon
- *Full moon:* Elder Dragon Moon
- *Crystal:* Clear quartz
- *Ritual candles:* Silver and white
- *Energy focus:* Family, both blood and chosen. Petition the dragons for blessings of goodness and prosperity for your loved ones.

## Third Winter Lunar Cycle

- *New moon:* Awakening Dragon Moon
- *Full moon:* Vision Dragon Moon
- *Crystal:* Clear quartz
- *Ritual candles:* Blue and silver
- *Energy focus:* Personal creative growth and inspiration

## First Spring Lunar Cycle

- *New moon:* Awakening Dragon Moon
- *Full moon:* Maiden Dragon Moon
- *Crystal:* Rose quartz (or clear quartz as a substitute)
- *Ritual candles:* Pink and yellow
- *Energy focus:* Planting the seeds for a bountiful return. This might be a working for an actual garden, a personal goal, or simply the hope for a beautiful and peaceful spring.

## Second Spring Lunar Cycle

- *New moon:* Awakening Dragon Moon
- *Full moon:* Fertility Dragon Moon
- *Crystal:* Rose quartz (or clear quartz as a substitute)
- *Ritual candles:* Pink and yellow
- *Energy focus:* Fertility—this can be either physical or figurative fertility.

## Third Spring Lunar Cycle

- *New moon:* Sky Dragon Moon
- *Full moon:* Dream Dragon Moon
- *Crystal:* Rose quartz (or clear quartz as a substitute)
- *Ritual candles:* Pink and yellow
- *Energy focus:* Manifesting dreams

### First Summer Lunar Cycle

- *New moon:* Sky Dragon Moon
- *Full moon:* Rain Dragon Moon
- *Crystal:* Citrine quartz (or clear quartz as a substitute)
- *Ritual candles:* Orange and red
- *Energy focus:* Replenishment

### Second Summer Lunar Cycle

- *New moon:* Sky Dragon Moon
- *Full moon:* Storm Dragon Moon
- *Crystal:* Citrine quartz (or clear quartz as a substitute)
- *Ritual candles:* Red and orange
- *Energy focus:* Cleansing

### Third Summer Lunar Cycle

- *New moon:* Awakening Dragon Moon
- *Full moon:* Harvest Dragon Moon
- *Crystal:* Citrine quartz (or clear quartz as a substitute)
- *Ritual candles:* Orange and red
- *Energy focus:* Harvest

### First Autumnal Lunar Cycle

- *New moon:* Arrow Dragon Moon
- *Full moon:* Hunter Dragon Moon
- *Crystal:* Smoky quartz (or clear quartz as a substitute)
- *Ritual candles:* Brown and orange
- *Energy focus:* Seeking and finding

### Second Autumnal Lunar Cycle

- *New moon:* Infant Dragon Moon
- *Full moon:* Ancestor Dragon Moon

- *Crystal:* Smoky quartz (or clear quartz as a substitute)
- *Ritual candles:* Brown and orange
- *Energy focus:* Honoring ancestors

### Third Autumnal Lunar Cycle

- *New moon:* Bounty Dragon Moon
- *Full moon:* Gratitude Dragon Moon
- *Crystal:* Smoky quartz (or clear quartz as a substitute)
- *Ritual candles:* Brown and orange
- *Energy focus:* Gratitude

### Thirteenth Lunar Cycle

- *New moon:* Hidden Dragon Moon
- *Full moon:* Shadow Dragon Moon
- *Crystal:* Clear quartz
- *Ritual candles:* Silver and white
- *Energy focus:* Honoring the moon shadow dragon

## MEDITATION: MOON SHADOW DRAGON

This meditation will introduce you to another lunar dragon, one that I call the moon shadow dragon.

Locate an area that is quiet and where you will not be disturbed. This can be outside or inside; the most important consideration for these meditations is that you are comfortable and feel safe. Be sure to wear clothing that does not hinder your movement and that the temperature and lighting are pleasant. Sit or lie down, whichever suits you, and close your eyes.

Breathe deeply. In and out. Concentrate on your breath as it enters your lungs, filling you with life, and then feel it exhale, leaving you energized.

Now, focus on one deep, slow breath to energize and clear your body. In and out. Another deep, slow breath to energize and clear your mind. In and out. Finally, another deep, slow breath to energize and clear your spirit.

Let the cares and concerns of the mundane world roll away from your neck … your shoulders … your arms … your fingers. Allow your back to relax, from your neck down, down, down to the base of your spine … and just breathe …

Allow your focus to rest behind your closed eyes as you feel your body relax completely. You are still. You are quiet.

In your mind's eye, see yourself on a rocky hillside. It is just becoming dark; the sun's light is just a memory of color in the west. The air is clear and fresh. The moon is full above you and shining brightly. The energy of this place, of this time, is solid, good, and strong.

You stand at the bottom slope of a tall, craggy mountain. As you look up, you see a path that leads up the mountain; it is a path that is familiar to you.

Begin walking upon the mountain path, slowly ascending. Each footstep is deliberate and sure. Your breathing is deep and satisfying.

Take a few more steps and you will see the familiar cave entrance in the mountain. Stand at the entrance and take a deep breath. Concentrate on the stillness.

Above the entrance, you see the outline of carved images begin to glow with a silvery light. As the moon's light grows stronger, the images become clear: a waxing crescent moon, a full moon, and a waning crescent moon.

You enter the cave with sure, deliberate steps. Focus on your breathing. Take slow, deep breaths. When you are calm and focused, a dragon's voice comes through the darkness:

*Welcome, Seeker! I am the moon shadow dragon.*

Continue to concentrate on your breathing. From the shadows, you see the outline of an enormous silvery-white dragon. She speaks to you again:

*Why seek you the moon shadow dragon?*

Respond in truth; certainly, you seek any wisdom that the moon shadow dragon is willing to share. Perhaps, you have something more specific as well. Take your time with this initial dialogue with the moon dragon.

*Come closer*, bids the moon shadow dragon.

Move closer to the dragon. Notice how her scales shine with luminescent color. Note that her claws are true silver and glisten with sharp edges. The moon dragon extends one of its claws toward you. The dragon places the claw just above your head. Almost instantly, the top of your head becomes warm. You feel a gentle nudge as energy from the dragon begins to mingle with your own energy.

*Place your right hand over my heart*, says the moon shadow dragon.

Gently place your right hand on the scales of the dragon's chest, just between her forelegs.

As the moon shadow dragon opens herself to the energy exchange, you first sense a great love emanating from her heart. This energy tingles delicately as it enters you; looking at your hand, it has a rosy pink glow surrounding it. Let the love fill you and comfort you. Take the time to fully immerse yourself in this gift of energy.

Above your head, a crown of silver energy has formed. The moon shadow dragon's claw is moving slowly in a clockwise direction. You hear the voice of the dragon as it sings:

*Far up above*
*With the stars on high*
*Lives a great dragon*
*Who is waiting in the sky.*
*What she waits for*
*Is a riddle in itself.*
*The answer awaits you.*
*Dare you seek the path?*

Take as much time as you need to experience the energy exchange with the moon shadow dragon. When you feel that you are ready to end this meditation, thank the moon shadow dragon for this communion and for the energy.

Take three deep breaths. You feel a shift in the energy around you. You begin to feel a bit heavier as you become more aware of your body.

Focus on the back of your eyes as you continue to breathe. Now, open your eyes. You have returned to your safe space in this world. You feel refreshed by this communion with the dragons.

## JOURNAL ENTRIES

For the meditation, the following journal entries are suggested:

1. Describe how the energy exchange felt between the dragon's claw and the crown of your head.

2. Was it surprising to initially feel love coming from the moon shadow dragon? Did you experience any other strong emotions from the connection?

3. How did the scales above her heart feel? Warm? Cool? Describe the experience in sensory detail.

## LUNAR DRAGON RITUAL EXERCISES

Lunar dragon ritual should be a smooth energetic communion between your spirit and the spirit of the celestial moon dragon. Riding the lunar energy cycle from new moon to full moon does take practice, though. In time, you will discover your own personal ritual tools and methods that will empower and enhance the energy exchange between you and the celestial dragons.

Use the rituals, dragon calls, recipes, and templates in this book to practice and eventually become a seasoned ritualist. At some point, with consistent ritual practice, you will probably feel a desire to write your own invocations or add more ritual tools as you sow the dragon's teeth. The following exercises are designed to aid you in that progression and encourage you to work with other aspects of celestial dragon energy.

### Compose a Lunar Ritual

Compose a lunar ritual that is designed to strengthen your relationship with the lunar dragon energy. Remember that your relationship with the dragons is based on trust and truth. Meditate on the ritual and record in your journal what you see, hear, and feel in your mind's eye. Here are some considerations for composing the ritual:

- Determine whether you will use only the full moon energy or the entire lunar cycle from new moon to full moon, which would be two rituals.

- Try chanting or even singing the dragon invocations and Dragon's Rune.

- Take the time to transform the words of your petition into a poem or song.

- Review your ritual and then visualize it during a meditation. Record and integrate any changes that come to you.

- Perform the ritual. Remember to record the experience in your journal.

### Creating Ritual Tools

Making your own ritual tools will add more of your energy to your dragon rituals. Here are a few suggestions for constructing ritual tools:

- *Candles:* Consider making or preparing candles that are especially for the deity and elemental dragons. Candle kits and supplies can be purchased from most hobby shops, and instructions can be found in libraries and online sources. The focus for the candles should be color and wax materials.
  - Deity dragon candle colors: For the deity dragons, I recommend silver and gold, but you will discover the colors that suit your personal rituals as you commune with the dragons.
  - Elemental dragon candle colors: Earth element candles should be browns or greens, possibly gray or black for stone. Fire element candles should be red or yellow. Water element candles

should be a shade of blue. Air element candles should be a shade of yellow. Purple is the color for spirit candles. White can always be substituted as needed, and it is not a bad idea to have some white candles on standby just in case.

## Personalize Your Altar

Personalize and enhance your ritual altar. You may feel the calling to add symbols, statuary, or other decoration to your altar for celestial rituals.

- *Symbols:* If you receive or discover a symbol that you want to incorporate into your lunar and celestial rituals, research the symbol to see if it is or has been used for ritual purposes. If you know other magickal practitioners, ask a trusted fellow ritualist if they recognize the symbol. Once you have determined that the symbol is a tool that you can use in your rituals, change your focus to how you want to use that symbol. Will you inscribe it onto a candle? Will you carve it onto your altar? Will you wear the symbol as a necklace or ring while in ritual?

## Sacred Statuary

If you have the talent to create your own statuary, consider yourself blessed, as you will be able to focus your energy into this tool from inception to ritual use. If, like me, you are obliged to purchase statuary for ritual, then research (yes, more research!) what you plan to buy and from where you plan to buy it. Even if you buy a piece from a festival and you know it was made with magickal intent, you will still need to energetically cleanse the statue. If you inherit statuary from another ritualist, you will need to cleanse it before you use it. No matter the origin of the ritual tool (unless you have made it yourself and been careful to only put magickal intent into the creation energy), you will need to cleanse all ritual tools before you use them. To cleanse, you can use incense, direct sunlight, or both. Do not use water or other liquid unless you are certain that the statue material will not be damaged. In general, avoid chemical cleansing unless the circumstances call for it.

**Ritual Decoration**

You may be inspired to use certain altar colors, candlestick holders, censers, or candles for lunar dragon rituals. Certainly, silver, gray, and white are associated with lunar energy and can make for a stunning altar. Consider crescent-shaped candlestick holders for new moon rituals and circular candlestick holders for full moon rituals. Perhaps purchase a plain censer and place a moon or dragon symbol upon it.

## LUNAR DRAGON MAGICK AND RITUAL OVERVIEW

The current of energy that runs between and connects the earth and the moon is powerful. Our body and spirit react with an intuitive sense of awareness to the position of the moon in relation to the earth. With practice, we can learn how to ritually connect with that lunar energy and form a cyclic alliance with the dragon energy of the moon.

The lunar dragon rituals in this chapter used the new and full phases of the moon's cycle. This cycle has the new moon ritual focusing on the seeker's petition, and the full moon ritual concludes the working with acknowledgment and thanksgiving. Using ritual over time, with much patience and diligent observation, you will intuitively and consciously learn the language of how spirit transmutes into the physical world.

## CHAPTER NINE

# DRAGON SPELLCASTING

If you look up the definition of a magick spell, you will discover more than a few varying responses. The words *conjure*, *enchantment*, and *hex* are likely to be listed as synonyms. If you ask an experienced spellcaster what a spell is, their response may differ as well.

For the dragon spellcasting technique described in this chapter, a spell is defined as a focused energy working that has a specific, desired outcome. As you will see, spells can be simple, or they can be elaborate and involve many components. Like the ritual template that was introduced in the preceding chapters, a spellcasting template is provided here as well.

Spells and rituals are similar esoteric workings. So, how does a spell differ from a ritual? A ritual might be a celebratory occasion or simple sacred space invoked for a quiet, contemplative meditation with the dragons. A spell does not require a ritual setting, although spells can and often are cast in sacred space. Your experiences will determine the best setting for your spellcasting and will reveal, sometimes through trial and error, what works for you and what does not.

A very specific purpose for spellcasting is a must, and you must be crystal clear with what that purpose is before you begin any energy work. The words of a chant or charm cannot be vague or imply multiple meanings. Practice speaking, singing, or writing what your desired outcome is. As you prepare to begin the practice of spellcasting with dragon magick, heed the wisdom of never causing harm to anyone or anything, including yourself. Let your purpose and words be guided by love and trust.

## THIRTEEN STEPS OF DRAGON SPELLCASTING

The template for spellcasting with dragon energy consists of thirteen steps. The steps begin at the end, so to speak, with what the result of the spellcasting is expected to be:

1. *Outcome:* Establish the desired result for the spellcasting

2. *Composition:* Create or review spell components

3. *Preparation:* Gather spell components

4. *Clearing:* Cleanse spellcasting area

5. *Activation:* Awaken spirit self and spell components

6. *Proclamation:* Announce intention to the dragon realms

7. *Chant or incantation:* Rouse energy for spellcasting

8. *Action:* Do acts specific to this spellcasting

9. *Conjuration:* Spell components merge

10. *Release:* Spell is cast

11. *Completion:* Spellcasting is concluded

12. *Manifestation:* Spellcasting elements begin to form into desired
   outcome

13. *Assessment:* Review spellcasting and results

## Outcome

Simply put, the outcome for the spellcasting is a very detailed answer to the questions, What is it that you desire? What do you want to happen? Start with a general statement and then narrow your purpose. For example, you may need a new vehicle. However, if you simply state or write, "I need a new vehicle," many outcomes are possible. You might receive a new bicycle as a present, or you might find a model car in the attic that you thought you had lost. Narrow down and focus on what you really want to happen; the details may seem meticulous at first, but it must be done.

Let us continue with the "new vehicle" example. Do you want to purchase or lease this vehicle? State clearly how you envision your role as the owner or driver of the vehicle. "Vehicle" is rather vague as well; be specific about exactly what it is that your needs require. Perhaps you need a multi-passenger vehicle. Maybe it is time for you to use a vehicle that is powered by electricity.

Make a list of the specific details that you want to manifest from the spell. You can work the list into a poem, song, or chant at a later time if you wish, or you can simply compose the list on paper and recite it during the spellcasting.

As you work through establishing the desired outcome, use creative visualization to see with your mind's eye the manifestation of your working as well. If a title or name for the spell comes to you during this time or later, record it in your journal.

## Composition

If you are going to cast a spell that has already been written, whether it is an ancient or modern spell, you should still use the thirteen steps of spellcasting to review and edit as necessary. Research the spell's origins: Has the spell been widely used? By whom? Is it limited to a certain magickal tradition? Is there any chance that the spell has been misused and brought harm to anyone or anything? All of these questions should be answered before you decide to put your energy into the spell. Furthermore, be sure that the spell aligns with your desired outcome, or if you are editing, use careful wording to change the spell's focus.

Your new spell should include directions for what to do and when. List the items that are needed. Be specific, as timing and focus are key to a successful spellcasting.

The lunar cycle is a key component for spellcasting in this template. The basic premise is that a spell that is trying to manifest should be cast during the new moon phase. The belief is that the spell will gain power as the moon's energy builds. For a spell that is attempting to banish, the casting should take place during the full moon phase. The waning lunar energy will work in tandem with the dismissive energy of your spell.

Preferably, you will have the time to work within the time frame of the lunar energy cycle. However, life happens, and occasionally you will find yourself preparing for a spellcasting that has to happen quickly. In these situations, use your intuition and ask the dragons for guidance. As you become more experienced as a dragon spellcaster, you will find what works for you and what does not. Your wisdom will come from these experiences. Remember them well.

If you want to convert your lists and notes into a poem, song, or chant that will become your incantation, now is the time. Record the words and then read them to yourself silently. Determine a rhythm for the words. Typically, a spell begins softly spoken and then gains volume and momentum as the energy is released. A proper verse type is not necessary to employ; however, some flavor of rhyme and cadence will assist greatly with the energy raising for the spell:

> *Come, dragons of sea and land.*
> *Join me now, hand in hand.*

As you compose the spell, be sure and pay attention to your mind's eye and note the colors, sounds, or words that come to you. Incorporate them into your spellcasting.

## Preparation

The spell has been composed, edited, or reviewed. The timing of the casting has been set. Gather the physical components for the spellcasting. Check the list multiple times and place the items where you can easily use them as needed.

Similar to ritual, you also want to prepare your spirit self. A ritual bath, shower, or dragon's breath bath is recommended. Wear loose, comfortable clothing. Make sure that your mind is clear of worries. You should feel relaxed and at peace as you begin the magickal work of spellcasting.

## Clearing

You have your spellcasting items arranged as needed and your higher self is awakening. You want to have full control over the energy in this space, so before you cast, you should energetically clear the area of any unnecessary or residual vibrations.

Stand in the center of the area, raise your arms above your head, and spread your feet slightly apart. Imagine a bright white light illuminating and enveloping your body and spreading outward. Imagine the light drives out any negative energy softly and completely. When you feel that only positive energy remains, allow the light to fade. Relax your body and return to a comfortable position.

## Activation

To activate the space for the upcoming energy build, light a candle. This single flame is a beacon to the dragon realms that a magickal working is imminent. If you have incense to burn or more candles to light, visualize each action like an "on" switch for energy to flow.

## Proclamation

You have the attention of the dragon realms. Now, you should declare what is going on and why you have activated this space for energy work. Speak the purpose of this spellcasting aloud with a firm and confident voice. Your proclamation should be clear, focused, and succinct.

## Incantation

The energy build for the spellcasting continues with the incantation. In this spellcasting template, the incantation is the audible portion of the spell that states precisely what is desired as the outcome of the spell. You may have written a poem or song, or your list may simply be announced with a particular cadence. Whichever method you use for this part of the spell, this is your magickal summons; speak with confidence. You may speak these words only once, or you may feel that repetition is necessary. You must use your intuition to decide. Speak your incantation clearly, and when it is done, pause a few moments to allow the energy of your words to resonate across the realms.

## Action

Acts specific to this spellcasting such as gestures, actions, and movement are next. You may choose to burn the paper that has the incantation written on it as a spell action. Certainly, the transformation of the paper by the burning flame is a viable and tactile energy release. You may choose to light a candle, incense, or both as a signal that the spell is unfolding. There may be a symbol whose power you wish to invoke, such as a rune or letter. A bell, drum, or other musical instrument can be used to further add to the spell's power.

## Conjuration

Your spellcasting efforts are now nearly ready for release. The proclamation, incantation, and actions are done. The table, so to speak, is set for the main event. It is your responsibility to gather the energy that has been building, focus it, and then release it to the realms of spirit so that manifestation can take place. Keep in mind, the manifestation is going to take place in the spirit realms and in the physical world.

If you are not already, take a standing position. Stretch your arms outward and to either side of your body. Place your feet slightly apart. Allow your body and spirit to touch the energy of your spell. Coax the energy to mingle. Allow it to swirl and bend as it takes the shape of the spell's focus. With gentle but firm control, hold the energy.

## Release

The energy for your spell is ready to be released for manifestation. The energy has probably taken a shape—perhaps a geometrical one, or it might be something more aligned with the spell's purpose. For instance, if this is a protection spell, the energy may form into the shape of a shield. To release the energy for manifestation in the spirit realm, nudge the energy toward the sky. Similar to a ritual energetic release, when you sense that the spell's energy is near the boundary between the physical and spiritual realms, release your hold. The energy will appear to dissipate into the ether.

## Completion

It is a good magickal practice to make it clear that your spellcasting work in this space is complete. You can announce this like you did the spell proclamation, or you can simply visualize the space becoming lighter and clearer. Extinguish any candles or other burning items. Clean and tidy the area, leaving no residual components that might interfere or send mixed signals to the spirit realms, where your spell is now manifesting.

## Manifestation

This template uses the lunar cycles to assist with the spell manifestation. So whether you are expelling energy with the waning moon or gathering energy with the waxing moon, the spell components and associated energy are beginning to form into your desired result. Likewise, if you have had to spellcast outside of the lunar cycle, there is still a manifestation period, albeit a brief one, for the energy.

In the physical world, you should be mindful that the manifestation is occurring. Anticipate and prepare for your spell's energy to follow its intended course. In other words, if you have cast a spell to find a new place of employment, update your resume and start applying to jobs. If your spell only requires that you wait patiently, then certainly avoid any actions that would work against your desired outcome.

There may not necessarily be a moment when you realize that the spell is complete, or the conclusion of the magickal working may be loud and clear. This will differ from spell to spell and certainly from spellcaster to spellcaster. What you experience is what becomes the wisdom you use for future esoteric work.

## Assessment

Your assessment really should begin after you have released the energy of the spell. As soon as possible, record how you felt during the spellcasting. Did your body grow hot or cold at any point? What did you hear, if anything, after you voiced the incantation? What shape did the spell's energy take before it joined with the spirit realm for manifestation? Record any and all things that come to you in the time following the actual casting of the spell. Hindsight is indeed an invaluable tool for the wise spellcaster.

When the energy of the spell has manifested into the desired outcome, record that result as well. When did you sense that the spell was complete? Write down the day, time, and any celestial correspondences. Do you feel that the spell was a success? Why?

You may find that what has manifested is not quite what you wanted or expected. You may even feel that nothing manifested at all. First, expect and accept that spells do go awry. Occasionally a spell is so misdirected that only chaos results. Rarely, ill-formed spells can cause harm. All of these outcomes are possible. Your experience is your future wisdom, so you are obligated to investigate every outcome. Seek the advice of spellcasters whom you respect. Abandon anything that causes harm. Embrace the spell and spell components that work for you.

## SPELLCASTING MODEL: SPELL FOR SAFE TRAVEL

Using this thirteen-step template, you can cast a spell for whatever you seek. Here is a spellcasting example that I use for safe travel. To engage dragon energy for this spell, I use a simple chant combined with a rune stave. I work closely with the Scandinavian dragon energy in my personal dragon practice, so the flavor, if you will, of my spells tends to be what I call the dragons of ice and snow. You can adjust the Scandinavian aspects of this spell to align with the dragon energy that works for you. For example, rather than using a Vegvisir rune stave, you might use an Egyptian hieroglyph or other esoteric symbol that represents movement.

### Outcome

The desired outcome for this spellcasting is that the traveler arrive safely to their destination without incident.

## Composition

This is my original spell for safe travel that uses a pattern of Norse runes made into a magickal symbol called a rune stave. A rune stave is a selected design of Norse runes fashioned into a circular symbol. The rune stave used for this spell is called Vegvisir.

For this spell, you will need a blue candle and to either draw the Vegvisir rune stave on a piece of paper or obtain a physical Vegvisir amulet.

*The Vegvisir rune stave*

## Preparation

Draw the rune stave or purchase or make an amulet of the rune stave. If drawn, put the rune stave on a piece of paper before the actual spellcasting. If using an amulet that was purchased or otherwise procured, cleanse it with incense before the working begins.

This is a spell where you will be *invoking* protective energy for the traveler, so it is best to use the *waxing* cycle of the lunar phase, as during this time the moon is gaining energetic momentum. If the travel is unexpected, the spell can be done in a timely manner and with necessary variation.

## Clearing

If you are at home, use your designated ritual area for spellcasting. If you are not able to use your personal sacred space, then simply visualize the details for this step in the spellcasting. Stand before your altar, raise your arms above your head, and spread your feet slightly apart. Visualize a bright, white light illuminating and enveloping your body and spreading outward. Imagine that the light removes any unneeded energy softly and completely.

## Activation

Light a light blue candle. Then visualize the ice and snow as a type of "on" switch that the spellcasting is beginning.

## Proclamation

*I invoke the protection of my dragon allies*
*so that I will arrive without incident or delay to [destination].*

## Incantation

*Dragons of the northlands,*
*I call upon you now.*
*Dragons of ice and snow,*
*See here the wayfinder.*
*May it guide me well.*
*May it hold me in the protection of the gods.*
*No storm or bad weather shall hinder me,*
*Even when I wander as Odin does.*

## Action

Hold the amulet or paper in your open right hand.

## Conjuration

Speak these words:

*See the wayfinder,*
*Here in my hand.*

*Journey companions,*
*The dragons and me.*
*Wanderer or traveler,*
*I am protected.*
*I will arrive at my destination*
*And return home again*
*Unharmed and whole.*

## Release

The energy that has been building from the incantation and conjuration is ready to be released. Nudge the energy into the spirit realm of the dragons of ice and snow. Visualize the spell moving into a landscape of blue ice and sparkling white snow, where dragons dwell in nearby caves.

## Completion

When you are done with the visualization, announce that the spellcasting has concluded by speaking, "It is done," and then extinguishing the flame of the candle. Keep the paper or amulet in a quiet place, such as your altar, during the manifestation phase.

## Manifestation

The spell's energy is intended to manifest into the rune stave. When the lunar cycle is complete or you sense that the spell is concluded, place the paper in a pocket of your clothing or wear the amulet. When the journey has concluded, safely burn the paper in a firesafe container on your altar. If you crafted your own amulet, you may continue to wear it or place it somewhere safe until it is needed again.

## Assessment

This spell has worked successfully for me and others on multiple occasions. Anytime you do this (or any) spell, record the experiences in your journal or spell book, if you have one. Conversely, rough travel experiences are rarely forgotten, so if the spell goes awry, I remember it well, as will you. Record those details for later investigation and alterations to the spell.

## SPELLCASTING MODEL: FINDING WHAT IS LOST

To engage dragon energy for assistance in finding something or someone who is lost or beyond your reach, I use a simple chant with a rune stave of my own making. I call upon the far-sight and wisdom of the dragons of ice and snow to aid me with a magickal petition for their aid.

### Outcome

The desired outcome for this spellcasting is that what is lost will be found.

### Composition

This is another of my spells that uses a Scandinavian rune stave (this one of my own making) that I have named the *Spurði*. *Spurði* roughly translates from Old Norse to English as "to hear of" or "learn of something." The stave is a combination of three Norse runes: Hagalaz, Mannaz, and Ingwaz, which are combined to look like this:

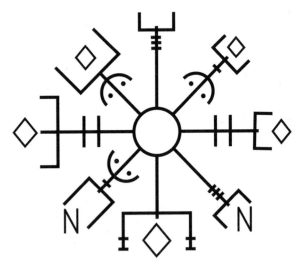

*The Spurði rune stave*

Gather your tools and other ritual needs, including a representation or drawing of the *Spurði* rune stave, the magickal incantation included here, and a blue candle.

## Preparation

Draw the rune stave on a piece of plain paper. This is a spell where you will *invoke* the seeing energy of the dragons, so use the *waxing* cycle of the lunar phase, as during this time the moon is gaining energetic momentum. If the item or person needs to be found in a more expeditious manner, the spell can be cast without regard to lunar cycle. However, the spellcaster should be mindful that the lunar energy will not be a consideration for the manifestation period.

## Clearing

If you are at home, use your designated ritual area for spellcasting. If you are not able to use your own sacred space, then simply visualize the details for this step in the spellcasting. Stand before the altar, raise your arms above your head, and spread your feet slightly apart. Visualize a bright white light illuminating and enveloping your body and spreading outward. Imagine that the light removes any unneeded energy softly and completely.

## Activation

Light a light blue candle, which symbolizes the ice and snow, as your "on" switch that the spellcasting is beginning.

## Proclamation

> *I invoke the energy of the dragons of ice and snow*
> *so that [object or person] can be found.*

## Incantation

> *Dragons of the northlands,*
> *I call upon you now.*
> *Dragons of ice and snow,*
> *See here my runes.*
> *I seek what cannot be found.*
> *I look for what I cannot see.*
> *I listen for that which has been silent.*

## Action

To invoke the vision and wisdom of the dragons into the *Spurði* rune stave, hold the paper with the rune stave in your open right hand.

## Conjuration

Speak the words:

> With the eyes of a dragon,
> With a bridge of strong scales,
> With my dragon allies and companions,
> I ask for the magick of the Spurði.
> Let me see what is hidden.
> Let me find what is lost.
> Let me hear what is silent.

Wait for seven breaths and speak these words:

> I see with the eyes of a dragon.
> I am a bridge of strength.
> I hunt with my dragon allies and companions.
> With the magick of the Spurði,
> I now see what is hidden.
> I will find what is lost.
> I will hear what is silent.

## Release

The energy should be ready to be released. Nudge the energy into the spirit realm of the dragons of ice and snow, a simple visualization of the energy moving into a landscape of blue ice and sparkling white snow where dragons dwell in nearby caves.

## Completion

Next, announce that the spellcasting has concluded by speaking, "It is done," and then extinguishing the flame of the candle. Place the paper on your altar.

Perform this spell at the same time every day until you have found what you seek.

## Manifestation

The spell's energy is intended to manifest into the rune stave. When the item or person has been found, burn the paper in a firesafe container at your altar.

## Assessment

This spell has also worked successfully for me many times. Be careful to include what was lost, when it was lost, and when and where it was found.

# SPELLCASTING MODEL:
# PETITION FOR EMPLOYMENT OR CAREER

The following "modern" dragon spell is from my own experience of working with dragon energy. This is a focused energy working where the dragons are called upon to act as guides and allies. To call upon the dragons to assist you when a new job or career path is desired, a simple chant combined with fourteen coins is used.

## Incantation

*Oh, ancient and mighty dragons,*
*Whose wisdom is a mighty gift,*
*I, [your name],*
*Ask that you lend your energy to what I do here.*
*I ask that the path to [new career or job] be open to me.*
*I ask that I receive the knowledge and means to become*
*[state new job position or career path].*
*I humbly request that our energy be joined,*
*That together our energy*
*Will result in [new job or career path].*
*It is done.*

Take fourteen coins, any kind will do, and place them on a surface that will not be disturbed for the next eight days. Place them in two rows of seven coins, parallel to each other.

Each day at the same time, stand over or near the coins and speak the incantation. After speaking, move the top two coins until they meet. Leave the coins touching each other.

Repeat this spell for seven days until all coins have been moved and are paired and touching. On the eighth day, take the coins and place them in a container. Go to a crossroads where you can safely toss the coins.

Stand in or near the crossroads, place the coins in your hands, and speak aloud:

*Oh, ancient and mighty dragons,*
*Your wisdom has been a mighty gift.*
*I, [your name],*
*Thank you for your gift and guidance.*
*You have opened the path to me for [new career or job].*
*I thank you for the knowledge and means to become*
*[state new job position or career path].*
*I am humbled by your gift.*
*It is done.*

After speaking the words, toss the coins into the air and let them fall where they may. It is done.

## CONNECTING TO THE MAGICKAL REALM OF THE DRAGONS

Take some time to go back and read through this chapter. In time, you will likely begin to compose your own dragon spells, amulets, and incantations. For now, add the following meditation to your dragon practice. Magick Dragon is meant to connect you more strongly to the spirit realms where your spells will manifest.

## MEDITATION: MAGICK DRAGON

Locate an area that is quiet and where you will not be disturbed. This can be outside or inside; the most important consideration for these meditations is that you are comfortable and feel safe. Be sure to wear clothing that does not hinder your movement and that the temperature and lighting are pleasant. Sit or lie down, whichever suits you, and close your eyes.

Breathe deeply. In and out. Concentrate on your breath as it enters your lungs, filling you with life, and then feel it exhale, leaving you energized.

Now, focus on one deep, slow breath to energize and clear your body. In and out. Another deep, slow breath to energize and clear your mind. In and out. Finally, another deep, slow breath to energize and clear your spirit.

Let the cares and concerns of the mundane world roll away from your neck... your shoulders... your arms... your fingers. Allow your back to relax, from your neck down, down, down to the base of your spine... and just breathe...

Allow your focus to rest behind your closed eyes as you feel your body relax completely. You are still. You are quiet.

In your mind's eye, see yourself on a rocky hillside. Is it twilight, or is it dawn? The world stands at the in-between time. You stand at the edge of a time without time—a place that is not a place. Yet it is all time and all space.

You stand at the bottom slope of a tall, craggy mountain. As you look up, you see a path that leads up the mountain; it is a path that is familiar to you.

Begin walking upon the mountain path, slowly ascending. Each footstep is deliberate and sure. Your breathing is deep and satisfying.

Take a few more steps and you will see the familiar cave entrance in the mountain. Stand at the entrance and take a deep breath. Concentrate on the stillness.

As you enter the cave, you sense that the air is alive with energy. You can hear voices whispering in the distance, and then, all at once, the whispering is just next to your ear.

*You have come to the place of magick and spell, Seeker.*
*Did you intend to come here?* whispers the voice.

Before you can respond, the room begins to swirl with vibrant colors. Purple, blue, red, yellow... every color and shade begins to dance in the air like ribbons.

*Ah, well, the magick has begun!*
*Sit here, be still, and listen!*

A small, three-legged stool appears beside you.

*Sit!*

Take a seat on the stool and concentrate again on your breathing.

Observe as the ribbons of color begin to join and form shapes. You see a range of craggy mountains, a single leaf, a newborn infant, a bowl of food … as you look around you, hundreds and hundreds of images are forming.

*These are the petitions from your world.*
*They are sent to the dragon realm*
*For us to consider, Seeker.*
*Know that I am the magick dragon,*
*One of many,*
*And we act as the gatekeepers for the realm of spells.*

You still do not see the dragon, yet you sense its presence very close to you. If you have questions for the dragon, ask them and wait patiently for a reply.

Take as much time as you need and experience the realm of dragon magick. When you feel that you are ready to end this meditation, thank the magick dragon for this communion and knowledge.

Take three deep breaths. You feel a shift in the energy around you. You begin to feel a bit heavier as you become more aware of your body.

Focus on the back of your eyes as you continue to breathe. Now, open your eyes. You have returned to your safe space in this world. You feel refreshed by this communion with the dragons.

## JOURNAL ENTRIES

For this meditation, the following journal entries are suggested:

1. Describe the images of the petitions that you saw. What color were they? Do you think that they were visualizations from our world? Did you see any writing?

2. How did it feel to be sitting in the midst of magickal energy? Describe the sensation using your five senses. What did it smell like? What did you hear?

## DRAGON SPELLCASTING OVERVIEW

This chapter introduced a dragon spellcasting technique and template that consists of thirteen steps. Though like a ritual energy working, spellcasting differs in that it is a focused energy working that has a specific, desired outcome. This focus is formed by the words and actions of the spellcaster. As we have seen, the words of a chant or charm cannot be vague or open-ended. Moreover, as you begin the practice of spellcasting with dragon magick, adopt the wisdom of never causing harm to anyone or anything, including yourself.

## CHAPTER TEN

# HARVESTING THE DRAGON'S TEETH

This book has gone in search of dragons, explored myths and lore, and studied dragon rituals and spells, all with the goal of establishing a working relationship with the dragons. Within the course of this relationship, you will transform your higher self and your life with the grace, power, and of the wisdom of the dragons. In this chapter, I will share how I practice sowing and harvesting the dragon's teeth with my own personal dragon practice. It is my hope that by sharing some of my personal dragon practices and dragon adventures that the dragon seeker may find a means to establish their own dragon magick routine.

## DRAGON ARCHETYPES

In my early dragon exploration, the guardian dragon archetypes presented themselves most often. I became well acquainted with the lore of the treasure guardians that we know as Beowulf's dragon and Fafnir. At first, I feared them. I saw them as frightening hoard beasts that would slay me easily and without a second thought.

Deep down, though, I sensed that there was something else to these dragons. Their devotion to their treasures was fierce, but in that devotion, I also felt a great love. I sensed that this love went beyond greed and gluttony, so I began to dig deeper.

Of course, delving into the likes of Beowulf's dragon and Fafnir placed me firmly in the energetic realms of both ice and snow. For some, it is odd, even uncomfortable, to honor the cold and ice. However, as I was to be reminded, snow and ice come from the sacred element of water. And for the Norse, from which these dragon tales originate, ice was considered a sacred and magickal element.

### Dragons of Ice and Snow

The realm of the ice dragon is indeed cold and hard. It is composed of frozen stone and vast caverns. These are old dragons whose tales and wisdom contain doorways to learning balance, the value of sacrifice, and the gift of initiation or spiritual rebirth.

Like me, most dragon seekers first encounter these dragons as horrific hoard-keepers—dragons who are deemed dangerous and certainly not to be trusted. Their sole purpose, we are told, is to accumulate a vast collection of valuables and guard it until they no longer can.

### The Hoard-Keepers of Scandinavia

There is more—so much more—to the guardian dragons, even the mighty hoard-keepers of Scandinavia. They are not mindless sentries, nor are they without intelligence. They are shapeshifters, magick users, initiators, and challengers. Their energy can aid the seeker in so many ways. The gift of their knowledge, wisdom, and even friendship is a powerful boon to the dragon magick practitioner.

## Fafnir: Hoard-Keeper and Shapeshifter

Upon the first reading or two of the lore of Fafnir the dragon, the story presents itself as a typical dragon slaying tale: A young male hero, Sigurd, is tasked with stealing the dragon's treasure. This thievery will require him to slay the beast. Sigurd's actions are seen as honorable since he will be ridding the world of incredible danger. As a shiny sidenote, Sigurd will likely become wealthy and famous.

Yet, Fafnir's story begins well before Sigurd seeks him deep in the forest. In fact, the story begins with Fafnir not as a dragon but as a dwarven prince. Fafnir was one of three royal brothers who desired gold and wealth above all other things. The brothers Otr, Regin, and Fafnir had the power to shapeshift into animal form. However, the story of the brothers, and eventually the tale of the dragon, is nothing short of tragic.

One of the brothers, Otr, is accidentally slain by the god Loki while in the form of an otter. Otr's father, Hreiðmarr, demands that Loki give gold as recompense for the murder, and it must be enough to fill the otter skin that was worn by his son.

Loki fills the otter skin with gold, but Hreiðmarr wants more. He desires Loki's ring, *Andvaranaut*, a magick ring whose purpose is to aid the wearer in finding more gold. Loki does give the king the ring, somewhat begrudgingly, and departs.

But the ring is cursed. It will drive the wearer to such greed that madness and death will overtake him. In the case of the dwarves, fighting over the treasure results in the death of Hreiðmarr, who decides that he will not share any of the gold with his two remaining sons.

After Hreiðmarr is slain, Fafnir transforms into a dragon, invokes the power of the rune stave the Helm of Awe, and takes control of the dwarven gold. Regin flees for his life and begins to plot his revenge.

Regin meets a young hero, Sigurd, and befriends him. The dwarf persuades Sigurd to seek Fafnir the dragon and slay the beast for the enormous treasure. Regin's greed still drives him, though. He is certainly no friend to Sigurd. The young man is the means to an end; Sigurd will be the slayer of the dragon, and then Regin will be the slayer of Sigurd.

Regin apparently has kept a close eye on his brother, Fafnir the dragon. The dwarf advises Sigurd that the dragon goes to a river every morning at dawn, and it should be there that Sigurd sets his trap.

Sigurd determines to dig a hole in the path that the dragon always takes to the river. Sigurd will hide in the hole and wait for the dragon. As the hero is digging the hole, the Norse Allfather, Odin, the one-eyed wanderer, appears to Sigurd disguised as an old man. Odin tells Sigurd to dig a second hole so that the dragon's venomous blood can flow away from Sigurd.

Sigurd digs a second hole, crawls into the first, and waits in silence for the dragon. Sigurd's attack is successful, as he stabs the beast with his sword, a death blow directly into Fafnir's heart.

As he dies, Fafnir speaks to Sigurd and engages his slayer in a lengthy dialogue. Fafnir's words when I read them in the Poetic Edda are tinged with a profound weariness and sadness. Fafnir warns Sigurd not once, but twice that the treasure is cursed:

> You think you are hearing words of hate,
> But what I tell you is true:
> The rings of gold, the fire-red treasure
> Will drag you down to your doom.

But Sigurd cannot be swayed from his purpose, so Fafnir tries again:

> Listen to me, Sigurd, and heed what I say—
> Ride home from here in haste!
> The fire-red treasure, the rings of gold,
> My hoard will be your bane.[18]

Fafnir dies, and Regin tells Sigurd to cut out the dragon's heart and roast it upon a spit. Regin plans to eat the dragon heart, and in doing so, gain the

---

18. Patricia Terry, trans., "The Lay of Fafnir," in *Poems of the Elder Edda* (Philadelphia: University of Pennsylvania Press, 1990), 153, 155.

knowledge and wisdom of dragons. Sigurd prepares a fire and begins to cook the dragon's heart.

What happens next is rather unexpected and fortuitous: Blood begins to bubble out from Fafnir's heart, and as Sigurd checks to see if the heart is fully cooked, he burns his thumb on the hot blood. Instinctively, Sigurd puts his injured thumb into his mouth. Immediately, Sigurd is gifted with the language of beasts. He is alarmed when he hears nearby birds yelling a message of warning: Regin plans to kill him. Dismayed but still determined, Sigurd slays Regin that night. He further curses himself when he claims the treasure as his own.

## Fafnir: Guardian and Initiator

Now, let us revisit the story of Fafnir from an esoteric viewpoint and apply the concept of sacrifice and synergy.

Rather than an evil dwarf who has killed his father, banished his brother, and shapeshifted into an equally evil dragon, imagine Fafnir as a spiritually connected individual who desires to advance his knowledge and wisdom. To attain those things, he must face the trials of such a path. Undoubtedly, that path will involve sacrifices.

Perhaps Fafnir did lose his father and brother during his youth, or their "deaths" could be spiritual in nature. Rather than being a kin slayer, Fafnir may well have been a witness to their transformation; he may even have facilitated or assisted with his family's spiritual practices. The brothers and father were shapeshifters, and this type of transformation is usually a talent that is learned after many years of spiritual practice. So it is likely that this royal family was gifted with the talent of shapeshifting.

When Fafnir changes into his dragon form, he becomes famous for his knowledge and insight. Even Sigurd says so to Fafnir as the dragon is dying:

> *Tell me, Fafnir, famed for your wisdom—*
> *I know you've learned much lore,*
> *What Norns will help women in their need*
> *Before they give birth?*

Fafnir answers him, and Sigurd goes on:

> *Tell me, Fafnir, famed for your wisdom—*
> *I know you've learned much lore,*
> *What is the island where blood will flow*
> *When Gods and the fire-giant fight?*[19]

Our alternative view of Sigurd and the dragon must also explore the possibility that Sigurd was not seeking to kill a monster and gain a vast fortune. Think of Sigurd as a seeker of dragons rather than a hunter of dragons. Consider that Sigurd, not unlike the young Fafnir, was on his own spiritual path in search of knowledge and wisdom. Where better to seek such things than from a dragon "famed" for his wisdom and lore?

Remember that Sigurd was advised by two individuals to dig holes into the earth. One hole was for him to await the arrival of the dragon; the second hole was to catch whatever might bring harm to the seeker. This imagery echoes a uterus. In an esoteric way, Sigurd is waiting within the womb of the earth mother. The seeker has entered the womb of the earth dragon and is waiting to be reborn. In many esoteric traditions, this is known as an initiation into the Great Mysteries.

The dialogue between Fafnir and Sigurd as the dragon "dies" is an oral representation of the esoteric changes and knowledge transfer that is occurring within them both. There is a rhythm and cadence to the dialogue that is not unlike that of a spell. In fact, the pattern of the dialogue is very closely aligned with what the Norse skalds used to compose and perform and is called *fornyrðislag*, which translates to "the ancient way of words." It is my belief that this "way of ancient words" was and is much more than simply a form of poetic verse; this weaving of words is a tool that was, and still can be, used to transform language into energy.

Finally, once the "dialogue" between the initiator and petitioner is complete, Sigurd is presented with the task of cooking the dragon's heart. Here, the dragon's heart is not a physical muscle, but instead symbolizes the integration between the physical and the spiritual. Sigurd is being challenged to

---

19. Terry, "The Lay of Fafnir," 154.

demonstrate his ability to transform energy. This test is a crucial part of his initiation; he is first aware of his success when he begins to understand the birds' words of warning.

This esoteric interpretation of the lore of Fafnir and Sigurd reveals a tale quite different from the usual dragon slaying story. As you study other dragon lore, remember to dig down and look beyond the physical descriptions. You will likely find that there is so much more to discover.

### Beowulf's Dragon: Fire Dragon, Protector, and Initiator

Much like Fafnir in the tale with Sigurd and Regin, the dragon in the epic poem *Beowulf* is also an initiator. In the poem, the old king, once a young hero, must face the wrath of a fire dragon who is ravaging the lands. The dragon has been enraged by the theft of a single stolen goblet by a poor, ignorant peasant.

Beowulf determines to face the angry dragon, and rather than take an army, he chooses eleven warriors and the thief who stole the goblet to accompany him in his grim purpose. Along with Beowulf, they number thirteen as they approach the dragon's lair.

The fires of the dragon frighten the warriors so badly that they do the unthinkable: they abandon their king, Beowulf, and hide in the nearby woods. A lone warrior, Wiglaf, enters the dragon's lair to assist Beowulf.

Wiglaf finds Beowulf wounded and near to death as the dragon attacks again. Together, the two warriors vanquish the beast despite the deadly venom and hot flame. Beowulf, though, has been mortally wounded. He gifts his armor to Wiglaf and asks to see the dragon's treasure before he dies. As he gazes upon the jewels and gold, the old king's broken body expires.

In an esoteric translation of Beowulf's encounter with the dragon, the old king symbolizes the wise man whose time has come to take the spiritual journey into the next world and away from this one. Before doing so, he must formally proclaim his successor and ensure that the proper rites are followed for a smooth transition of power and knowledge.

The theft of the goblet can be seen as the first step in a ritual for a passing of power from a wise teacher to his deserved apprentice. The "thief" is wily and clever in his act of stealing the dragon's cup. Yet, he is also selfish and destructive. He is the beginning of chaos and an initiator of change. This figure is often seen as the innocent fool.

Beowulf senses the release of chaos and hears the call of the dragon. The old sage knows that the time has come for his and the dragon's transformation. He chooses who will witness this rite of passage, and into the dragon's lair he goes. Again, the cave in the earth is symbolic of the womb and rebirth. Beowulf's dragon already dwells in the earth's womb with a treasure trove of knowledge, power, and wisdom. Beowulf enters the womb, and the shifting of energy causes the earth to rumble and shake.

Birth can often be violent and painful; for both Beowulf and the dragon, this is true. Their battle is an esoteric exchange of energy that contains memories and emotions. Finally, as the transfer between them nears completion, Wiglaf enters the womb to lend his energy to the rite. Wiglaf's successful initiation is symbolized by the gifts that Beowulf and the dragon give him. Beowulf's armor is a symbol that Wiglaf will replace him as the wise man and leader for their people. The items in the dragon's lair come to Wiglaf and his people and symbolize that with Beowulf and the dragon's sacrifice, peace and balance again prevail.

## PRACTICING BALANCE

One aspect of my personal dragon practice is a daily connection with and contribution to balance: the balance of my own personal life, the balance of my home, and the balance of the cosmos. This practice involves several Norse dragons—dragons of ice and snow—and their energies.

### Jormungandr: World Serpent

I first connect with the Norse world dragon Jormungandr, who is often portrayed visually as a sea serpent, but the ocean is not his only home. Jormungandr can and does engage with the element of water, but he has the power, knowledge, and mastery of all the elements. This dragon is the child of the Norse god of mischief, Loki, and a giant named Angrboða. Jormungandr was thrown into the ocean by Odin, and there he became a magnificent and massive creature. When he fully matured, he encircled the world with his body and assumed the vibration of stillness. He then took his tail into his mouth and became the beginning, the end, and the in-between. In a word, Jormungandr became infinity.

To connect with Jormungandr, I stand with my legs slightly apart and my arms outstretched. Closing my eyes, I reach deep within myself for a place of stillness and peace. I keep my breathing even with deep breaths. I call to Jormungandr in a slow monotone:

> *World Dragon, I, [your name], am here.*
> *I am still.*
> *I am at peace.*
> *Allow my energy to join with yours*
> *So that together we hold the balance,*
> *We keep the tension,*
> *So that the worlds are in harmony.*
> *It is done.*

The connection with Jormungandr allows me to contribute to the balance of the world. Through this connection, I can touch the cosmos and acknowledge the other components that contribute to or act against the balance. The next step in my balance practice is to acknowledge Nidhogg, a Norse chaos dragon.

## Nidhogg: Chaos Dragon, Biter, and Mover

Nidhogg is a Norse dragon whose purpose is to gnaw at the roots of Yggdrasil, an ash tree at the center of Norse cosmology. It is the Yggdrasil that Jormungandr encircles in most visual representations. Nidhogg's name literally means "curse striker" or "he who has malice," and every day the dragon bites and tears at the roots of the Yggdrasil, also called the World Tree. His actions cause a disturbance in the cosmos, which echoes outward. It is my belief that Jormungandr's coils around Yggdrasil hold Nidhogg's chaos at bay.

To connect with Nidhogg, I bring my arms inward across my chest and bring my legs close together. With my eyes still closed, I visualize Yggdrasil with Jormungandr wrapped protectively around it. I keep breathing slowly and with deep breaths. I visualize Nidhogg gnawing at the roots of Yggdrasil. I call to Nidhogg in a whisper:

*Nidhogg, I, [your name], am here.*
*Hear me:*
*You should be still.*
*You should be at peace.*
*Calm your mischief.*
*Soften your malice.*
*See the tension.*
*The worlds are in harmony.*
*It is done.*

The connection with Nidhogg allows me to safely acknowledge the chaos in the world and encourage the chaos to diminish, but also know that it cannot be banished. I am still able to touch the World Tree and nourish that connection. The next step in my balance practice is to bring that energy into my own personal life and home.

## Achieving Balance

Now that I have connected with the energy of Jormungandr and Nidhogg, I will bring the balance back home. I place my arms at my side with one foot slightly forward. I visualize Nidhogg gnawing at the things that I see as interference in my life while Jormungandr coils around me protectively. I speak quietly:

*Jormungandr,*
*Nidhogg,*
*Ancient and honored dragons of ice and snow.*
*I, [your name], call to you.*
*Help me bring peace to my home.*
*Allow me to bring balance to my life.*
*Gift me the strength and wisdom*
*So that together we can hold the balance,*
*We can keep the tension,*
*So that the worlds are in harmony.*
*It is done.*

## USING THE FUTHARK RUNES TO COMMUNICATE
## WITH THE DRAGONS OF ICE AND SNOW

While working with my ice and snow dragon companions, I discovered that the Futhark runes are an excellent method for directly communicating with them, as illustrated in the spellcasting chapter. Most likely, this is because these dragon spirits were birthed and still dwell in the same energy as the Northern wisdom of the runes.

The Futhark runes are amazing divining tools. If the runes call to you at all, I urge you to research and work with them regularly. I use the runes simply because I know that these runes were won by the Norse god Odin through sacrifice born from a great desire for knowledge. After piercing himself with a spear, Odin hung from the World Tree, bleeding and suffering. After nine days and nights, Odin cried out when he received the knowledge of the runes.

Odin then gifted the knowledge of the runes to humans. The runes were used in everyday writings by the Norse and Germanic tribal people as well as on runestones. Runes were (and still are) also used to divine messages from the gods and to communicate with the spirit realm.

## CREATING A SET OF DRAGON RUNESTONES

Viking runestones are standing stones with runes and drawings that honor a hero, a god, or act as funerary memorials. Futhark runes were drawn onto the stones in color and typically declare an event or triumph. In my personal practice, I have my own flavor of runestone, called dragon stones, that I use for divination and petitionary magick.

For making your own set of dragon runestones, a stone commonly called red tiger's eye is a good choice. Red tiger's eye stones are not as commonly found as the golden tiger's eye, but they can be located for bulk purchase in many esoteric shops, both physical and online. There are twenty-four Futhark runes, so you will need twenty-four stones.

The red tiger's eye, which will become dragon's eye stones, are beautiful dark red stones with darker lines throughout. When you get your stones, first clear them of any energies from those who may have handled them prior to you. To do this, simply run clear, cold water over the stones for 10–15 minutes and allow them to dry in the sunlight.

When you are ready to transform the stones into dragon runestones, gather your stones, find a quiet spot, and light some incense, a candle, or both. You are going to need a gold or silver marker as well. Concentrate on the stones and select one that catches your attention or calls to you. Hold that stone in your cupped hands and clear your mind. Wait for a Futhark rune to materialize in your mind's eye.

When the Futhark rune appears, give your thanks, and then concentrate on the dragon meaning of the rune. Visualize the rune flaming into the red stone. Take the silver or gold marker and draw the dragon rune onto the dragon stone. Continue this process until you have a full set of dragon runestones.

What follows now is an interpretation of the dragon runestones using the Futhark runes. Each Futhark rune is given a dragon runestone meaning for both inverted and upright positions. To "see" the dragon runestones, an upright Futhark rune should be rotated 90 degrees to the right. For the inverted dragon rune, an upright Futhark rune should be rotated 90 degrees to the left.

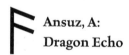

**Ansuz, A:**
**Dragon Echo**

*Futhark rune meaning:* Communication, understanding, inspiration

*Dragon rune:* Dragon Echo

*Dragon rune meaning:* There is one emulating the actions of another; ancestral or family memories are passed on.

*Dragon rune inverted:* Beware the one who mimics with false flattery. Some memories may be clouded. Seek clarity.

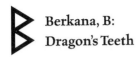 **Berkana, B:**
**Dragon's Teeth**

*Futhark rune meaning:* Powerful birth and rebirth

*Dragon rune name:* Dragon's Teeth

*Dragon rune meaning:* Marked by the dragon, one who sows the dragon's
teeth; significant change taking place now or will be very soon.

*Dragon rune inverted:* The path is blocked; it is a dead end with no way forward. The way is shut.

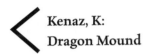 **Kenaz, K:**
**Dragon Mound**

*Futhark rune meaning:* Knowledge, understanding, learning

*Dragon rune name:* Dragon Mound

*Dragon rune meaning:* This is a place that houses vast stores of knowledge—
a cathedral of scrolls, tomes, maps, and other sources of wisdom.

*Dragon rune inverted:* A gaping hole in logic or reasoning. Reexamine situation and method to determine next steps.

 **Dagaz, D:**
**Dragon Grace**

*Futhark rune meaning:* Stability between opposites, balance, truce

*Dragon rune name:* Dragon Grace

*Dragon rune meaning:* A meeting of earth and sky or strength and intellect
that results in balance.

*Dragon rune inverted:* No inverted dragon rune—same meaning as upright
dragon rune.

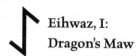 **Eihwaz, I:**
**Dragon's Maw**

*Futhark rune meaning:* Strength

*Dragon rune name:* Dragon's Maw

*Dragon rune meaning:* The means to a new experience is open; a teacher or mentor is willing and ready.

*Dragon rune inverted:* No inverted dragon rune—same meaning as upright dragon rune.

 **Fehu, F:**
**Dragon Flight**

*Futhark rune meaning:* Wealth, abundance, and security

*Dragon rune name:* Dragon Flight

*Dragon rune meaning:* Travel (by air most likely); probably involves companion, dragon ally, or both.

*Dragon rune inverted:* No inverted dragon rune—same meaning as upright dragon rune.

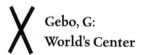 **Gebo, G:**
**World's Center**

*Futhark rune meaning:* Partnership, generosity, relationships

*Dragon rune name:* World Center

*Dragon rune meaning:* A convergence has been reached; physical, mental, or spiritual—a balance state of harmonious stillness pervades the situation.

*Dragon rune inverted:* No inverted dragon rune—same meaning as upright dragon rune.

# ᚺ Hagalaz, H:
## Dragon Bridge

*Futhark rune meaning:* Power and alertness

*Dragon rune name:* Dragon Bridge

*Dragon rune meaning:* A narrow and dangerous bridge exists between two paths; the path is open, but use skill and caution to cross.

*Dragon rune inverted:* No inverted dragon rune—same meaning as upright dragon rune.

# ᛁ Isa, I:
## Dragon Slumber

*Futhark rune meaning:* Stillness, waiting

*Dragon rune name:* Dragon Slumber

*Dragon rune meaning:* A period of stillness pervades. Rest, be at peace, wait patiently for the way to open.

*Dragon rune inverted:* No inverted dragon rune—same meaning as upright dragon rune.

# ᛃ Jera, J:
## Dancing Dragon

*Futhark rune meaning:* Cycle of life

*Dragon rune name:* Dancing Dragon

*Dragon rune meaning:* There is reason to celebrate; the dragons are dancing; success achieved followed by prosperity.

*Dragon rune inverted:* No inverted dragon rune—same meaning as upright dragon rune.

**Laguz, L:**
**Dragon Force**

*Futhark rune meaning:* Power of moving water

*Dragon rune name:* Dragon Force

*Dragon rune meaning:* The means to "power through" a difficult situation or predicament are available; keep moving; push through.

*Dragon rune inverted:* Something has a firm grip and is hindering progress; an undesired element is fastened tightly; parasite.

**Ehwaz, E:**
**Dragon Power**

*Futhark rune meaning:* Progress, motion

*Dragon rune name:* Dragon Power

*Dragon rune meaning:* A source of power and energy is available and ready to be tapped; a new skill or ability is ready to be harnessed.

*Dragon rune inverted:* No inverted dragon rune—same meaning as upright dragon rune.

**Mannaz, M:**
**Dragon Ally**

*Futhark rune meaning:* Man at his fullest potential

*Dragon rune name:* Dragon Ally

*Dragon rune meaning:* Collaboration; partnership; meeting of equals; creative alliance formed.

*Dragon rune inverted:* Be cautious with proposed collaboration(s); a partnership is out of balance.

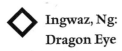 **Naudhiz, N:**
**Dragon Barrier**

*Futhark rune meaning:* Restrictive need or want

*Dragon rune name:* Dragon Barrier

*Dragon rune meaning:* Balance has been disrupted; flow is hindered.

*Dragon rune inverted:* No inverted dragon rune—same meaning as upright dragon rune.

 **Ingwaz, Ng:**
**Dragon Eye**

*Futhark rune meaning:* Fertility, growth

*Dragon rune name:* Dragon Eye

*Dragon rune meaning:* The path is clear.

*Dragon rune inverted:* No inverted dragon rune—same meaning as upright dragon rune.

**Othala, O:**
**Sea Dragon**

*Futhark rune meaning:* Inheritance, genetics

*Dragon rune name:* Sea Dragon

*Dragon rune meaning:* There are two ways to enter; both are open; keep moving.

*Dragon rune inverted:* Look at recent past; re-evaluate current direction.

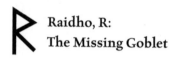

## Perthro, P:
## Dragon Ground

*Futhark rune meaning:* Secret and initiation

*Dragon rune name:* Dragon Ground

*Dragon rune meaning:* A common ground or mutual agreement is close; the goal is near to completion but requires cooperation with another.

*Dragon rune inverted:* A partnership or cooperative endeavor has gone awry; differing points of view or opinions result in different paths.

## Raidho, R:
## The Missing Goblet

*Futhark rune meaning:* The wheel, focus

*Dragon rune name:* The Missing Goblet

*Dragon rune meaning:* Something has been wrongfully taken; mistakes must be corrected; look for the missing piece of the mystery.

*Dragon rune inverted:* Entry into what is desired will be through a broken door; the hidden keyhole; a secret wall.

## Sowilo, S:
## Dragon Star

*Futhark rune meaning:* A light in the dark, the sun

*Dragon rune name:* Dragon Star

*Dragon rune meaning:* The darkness was indeed deep and impenetrable, but there is light ahead and ascension toward the sky.

*Dragon rune inverted:* No inverted dragon rune—same meaning as upright dragon rune.

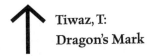 Tiwaz, T:
**Dragon's Mark**

*Futhark rune meaning:* Warrior energy

*Dragon rune name:* Dragon's Mark

*Dragon rune meaning:* All is ready for advancement; projects will proceed; journeys will begin; all is on target.

*Dragon rune inverted:* Use hindsight; take a few steps back; re-evaluate.

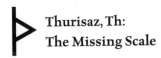 Thurisaz, Th:
**The Missing Scale**

*Futhark rune meaning:* Conflict, catharsis, regeneration

*Dragon rune name:* The Missing Scale

*Dragon rune meaning:* A weakness exists that has the potential to cause great harm; wound that needs healing.

*Dragon rune inverted:* A solution exists, but it seems small and insignificant; watch the horizon for clues.

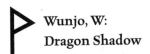 Wunjo, W:
**Dragon Shadow**

*Futhark rune meaning:* Fellowship

*Dragon rune name:* Dragon Shadow

*Dragon rune meaning:* What is needed lies in shadow; courage to achieve it; there is another path that is darker but leads to the same goal.

*Dragon rune inverted:* Seeker has completed an enlightening experience, possibly a trip or visit, or a great success was just recently celebrated. The road ahead awaits, but for now, the seeker is on a plateau of sorts.

 **Algiz, Z:**
**Dragon Wings**

*Futhark rune meaning:* Higher spiritual awareness

*Dragon rune name:* Dragon Wings

*Dragon rune meaning:* A state of higher vibration and spiritual awareness has been reached or is very close to being achieved.

*Dragon rune inverted:* What has been gained is ready to be transitioned. Let loose and fly.

**Uruz, U:**
**Dragon Ship**

*Futhark rune meaning:* Strength, tenacity, courage

*Dragon rune name:* Dragon Ship

*Dragon rune meaning:* A means for advancement presents itself.

*Dragon rune inverted:* The vessel or method currently being utilized to move forward is in need of repair.

## USING THE DRAGON RUNESTONES

When you are ready to make the first query with your dragon allies, take your bag of dragon runestones into both hands. Clear your mind, take three deep breaths, and concentrate on your question. If you're in a private place, light a blue candle and burn some frankincense before casting the runes, then speak your query aloud. (If you are in a position where you must be discreet, visualize lighting a candle and incense, send your questions silently, and wait for a runestone image or images to manifest.)

When you feel that your query has been made clear and that the lines of communication are open between yourself and your dragon allies, move the bag of runestones to your nondominant hand. With your dominant hand, reach into the bag and wait for the runestones to react. For me, the dragon runestones that hold the answer to my query vibrate when they make contact with my fingers and sometimes become warm. For you, the energy may feel different. When ready, select the runestones that are reacting to you and place them on a flat surface.

Here are a few examples of recent queries that I have made to my dragon allies using the dragon runestones:

**Query:** Is the current vision of my next writing project a good one?

**Dragon Runestones:** Dragon Eye (Ingwaz) + Dragon Star (Sowilo) + Dragon Ship (Uruz) + Dragon Wings (Algiz)

**Dragon Message:** Path is clear + Light ahead after hard work or toil + The means for moving forward is ready + Advancement of spiritual awareness will be achieved

I interpreted the dragon message to mean that the project would require significant time and effort, but that everything I need is at hand. In the end, a new spiritual awareness will result for me and perhaps others as well.

**Query:** Is there a message from the dragons for me today?

**Dragon Runestones:** Sea Dragon (Othala) + Dragon Eye (Ingwaz) + Dragon Shadow (Wunjo) + Dragon Wings (Algiz) + Dragon Flight (Fehu)

**Dragon Message:** There are two ways to enter; both are open; keep moving + The path is clear + What is needed lies in shadow; courage to achieve it; there is another path that is darker, but leads to same goal + On target, ready to loose + Travel (by air most likely); probably involves companion, dragon ally, or both

I interpreted this rune casting as a message that there are multiple ways to do what must be done, but they are not yet known to me. To find the means, I need to be brave and ready to take my chance. Travel is involved, either physical or spiritual, and includes my dragon companions.

## MEDITATION: DRAGONS OF ICE AND SNOW

Now, we will connect with the dragons of ice and snow in a meditation.

Locate an area that is quiet and where you will not be disturbed. This can be outside or inside; the most important consideration for these meditations is that you are comfortable and feel safe. Be sure to wear clothing that does not hinder your movement and that the temperature and lighting are pleasant. Sit or lie down, whichever suits you, and close your eyes.

Breathe deeply. In and out. Concentrate on your breath as it enters your lungs, filling you with life, and then feel it exhale, leaving you energized.

Now, focus on one deep, slow breath to energize and clear your body. In and out. Another deep, slow breath to energize and clear your mind. In and out. Finally, another deep, slow breath to energize and clear your spirit.

Let the cares and concerns of the mundane world roll away from your neck... your shoulders... your arms... your fingers. Allow your back to relax, from your neck down, down, down to the base of your spine... and just breathe...

Allow your focus to rest behind your closed eyes as you feel your body relax completely. You are still. You are quiet.

In your mind's eye, see yourself on a rocky hillside. It is just becoming dark; the sun's light is just a memory of color in the west. The air is clear and fresh. The moon is full above you and shining brightly. The energy of this place, of this time, is solid, good, and strong.

You stand on a clear and smooth glacier of snow and ice that stretches to the horizon in all directions. As you look around, you realize that you are much farther up the mountain and off the usual path.

Choose one direction and take a single step. Take another. Then another. Make each footstep deliberate and sure.

Your breathing is deep and smooth.

Before you, there is a crevasse in the ice. Move to the edge and look down. There is a cave of ice and snow below you.

Take a deep breath. Concentrate on the stillness. Take your time and climb down carefully into the cave.

You enter a vast cave that has walls of blue ice and a dusting of snow on the floor. You sense and then observe the energy of the cave begin to swirl and move. In the center of the cave, a small but warm campfire appears and burns contentedly.

In the eastern quadrant of the cave, a young man dressed in leather armor materializes. A bloody sword lays near his feet. His brow is creased with deep thoughts. Walk to the campfire and kneel near it.

Stare into the flames and allow your gaze to soften. Hold that tension. As you do, you hear the whispers of other voices.

> *Here is the heart of the dragon.*
> *Here is a path to knowing.*
> *Sacrifice leads to gratitude.*
> *Behold one who has the key.*

The young hunter is now dressed in robes of white and has a silver crown upon his brow.

He offers you a silver bowl of hot, dark liquid. Take the bowl. If you desire, take a small drink of the liquid.

In the south, a great dragon takes shape. He is enormous and wears a war helm with runes inscribed upon it. He studies you closely.

> *Who are you?* the dragon asks.

Respond with your name.

> *Come closer,* the dragon says.

Go to the dragon. If you have questions for the dragon, ask them now. If you receive answers, remember them for recording in your journal later.

In the west, the figure of an old man appears. He is dressed in magnificent armor and wears a crown. As you study him, his form begins to swirl and change. He transforms into a red fire dragon.

In the north, a dragon rests in a state of perfect stillness as it encircles a tree. It slumbers quietly as tiny ripples of its muscles move in a clockwise direction around its coils.

If you wish, you may question the dragons or anything that you encounter in this cave. Take as much time as you need with the dragons of snow and ice.

*The time has come to return to your own world and your own time,*
an Ice Dragon announces.

Take three deep breaths. Concentrate on the back of your closed eyes. With your next breath, you feel a shift in the energy around you. You begin to feel a bit heavier as you become aware of your body.

You have returned to your safe and sacred space in this world. You feel refreshed by this communion with the dragons.

Take three deep breaths. You feel a shift in the energy around you. You begin to feel a bit heavier as you become more aware of your body.

Focus on the back of your eyes as you continue to breathe. Now, open your eyes. You have returned to your safe space in this world. You feel refreshed by this communion with the dragons.

## JOURNAL ENTRIES

For this meditation, the following journal entries are suggested:

1. How did you feel when you realized that you weren't on your usual path up the mountain?

2. What did it feel like to be on the vast glacier of snow and ice?

3. Who was the young man that you encountered in the east? What did the liquid in the silver bowl taste like, if you drank it?

4. Did you have a dialogue with the dragon in the south? Record as much as you can recall. Compare it to Sigurd's dialogue with Fafnir.

## HARVESTING THE DRAGON'S TEETH OVERVIEW

Within the pages of this book, you have searched for dragons, and you now have a firm foundation for working with dragon energy and establishing your own magickal dragon practice. You have evolved your spiritual self with the blessings of the wisdom of the dragons. You have sown and begun the harvesting of the dragon's teeth upon your own path.

Experience the Dragons of Ice and Snow meditation as many times as you wish. Use your journal to record any insights that may come to you.

When you feel that you are ready, continue with the conclusion as we celebrate harvesting the dragon's teeth!

# TRANSFORMATION THROUGH DRAGONS

My personal dragon practice has come a long way since my first dragon encounter with Puff the Magic Dragon. By exploring the dragon tales and connecting with dragon energy, I now have my own path to the dragon realms.

## DRAGON LORE

Search for all the dragon lore that you can find and read it. Then read it again. As we have seen, many if not most dragon mysteries are right there in the myths and folktales. Revisit those old tales, especially the dragon lore that inspired the spirit of this book: the sowing of the dragon's teeth by the Greek heroes Jason and Cadmus.

## TRANSFORMATION

Although Cadmus and Jason had different experiences with sowing the dragon's teeth, both were transformed from the encounter. The same can be said of Sigurd, Beowulf, and other "dragon slayers."

Yet, we have seen that these transformations are not physical death or the "end." By working with the dragons and witnessing these events, you have joined your energy to theirs. You did indeed sow the dragon's teeth. As a result, you are transforming.

## RITUAL AND MEDITATION

The meditations, rituals, and other workings included in this book were simple ones. Now that you have experienced them, you may be ready to try other, more complex energy workings.

The meditations in this text are a template that I use in my own practice. As you progress in your harvesting of the dragon's teeth, your meditations will undoubtedly change into what works best for you and your dragon companions.

Remember, when communing with the dragons, create a special area wherever you may be, and take the time to energetically cleanse that spot.

Now, a final meditation wherein you will begin to harvest what you have sown.

## MEDITATION: HARVESTING THE DRAGON'S TEETH

Locate a small area that is quiet and where you will not be disturbed. This can be outside or inside; the most important consideration for these meditations is that you are comfortable and feel safe. Be sure to wear clothing that does not hinder your movement and that the temperature and lighting are pleasant. Sit or lie down, whichever suits you, and close your eyes.

Breathe deeply. In and out. Concentrate on your breath as it enters your lungs, filling you with life, and then feel it exhale, leaving you energized.

Now, focus on one deep, slow breath to energize and clear your body. In and out. Another deep, slow breath to energize and clear your mind. In and out. Finally, another deep, slow breath to energize and clear your spirit.

Let the cares and concerns of the mundane world roll away from your neck…your shoulders…your arms…your fingers. Allow your back to relax, from your neck down, down, down to the base of your spine…and just breathe…

Allow your focus to rest behind your closed eyes as you feel your body relax completely. You are still. You are quiet.

In your mind's eye, see yourself on a rocky hillside. There are scatterings of dew-moistened grass. The air is clear and fresh. The sun is warm upon your face. The energy of this place, of this time, is solid, good, and strong.

You stand at the bottom slope of a tall, craggy mountain. As you look up, you see a path that leads up the mountain. You know this path. You have walked it many times.

Begin walking the path, slowly, slowly, slowly ascending. Each footstep is deliberate and sure. Your breathing is deep and satisfying.

Take a few more steps and you will see a cave entrance in the mountain. It is familiar and yet somehow different.

Take a deep breath and enter the cave.

Take three more deep breaths.

You hear a distant rumble. Before you lies a massive creature near a small, gurgling stream. The dragon raises its head, flicks its tongue, and then turns its gaze upon you.

*You have returned.*
*I am glad to see it.*
*This place is sacred,*
*And I am its guardian.*
*Speak your name*
*And declare why you have come.*

Bow your head and send your name. Tell the guardian dragon that you are a humble seeker.

The dragon continues to study you, its gaze piercing and unblinking.

*You were shown the path to this place,*
*And you have proven yourself worthy*
*Of harvesting what you have sown.*
*You know this place and can return,*
*And now you may venture elsewhere as your courage allows.*
*I am Ismenia, the Ancient.*

Take three more deep breaths. Concentrate on the back of your closed eyes. With your next breath, you feel a shift in the energy around you. You begin to feel a bit heavier as you become aware of your body.

When you open your eyes, you will have returned to your safe and sacred space in this world. You will feel refreshed by this communion with the dragons.

Now, one more deep breath ... and open your eyes.

## JOURNAL ENTRIES

For this meditation, the following journal entries are suggested:

1. Describe the Ismenian Dragon with sensory and visual details. You have now met an ancient guardian dragon. What knowledge and wisdom can you gain from this dragon?

2. The dragon has opened other caverns for you to explore. Will you? What will you seek?

## CONCLUSION

Experience the Harvesting the Dragon's Teeth meditation as many times as you wish. Use your journal to record any insights that may come to you. You have come to the end, which is, of course, just another beginning! May the dragons bless and protect you!

# APPENDIX A

---

# DRAGON OIL
# AND INCENSE RECIPES

This section of the book includes recipes for herbal baths, oils, and incenses for use in dragon rituals and other workings. The recipes included here have been used in solitary as well as group magickal workings. The practitioner looking to incorporate any of these are encouraged to use the ingredients listed as a base. Additional ingredients can be added to enhance a blend's attunement with the intention of the working.

Please remember to do a skin test prior to use of any herbal or oil concoctions that will come into contact with your skin. To test, place a small amount of the blended herbs or oils (including a carrier oil) on the inside of your elbow, cover with a bandage, and check in 24 hours. If you experience any soreness, redness, or irritation, do not use the blend.

## RITUAL BATH RECIPE

Combine the following dried herbs and flowers in a small muslin bag:

- 1 tbsp or 14.8 ml rose petals
- ½ tsp or 2.5 ml chamomile
- 1 tsp or 5 ml rosemary
- ½ tsp or 2.5 ml peppermint

- 1 tbsp or 14.8 ml lavender
- ½ tsp or 2.5 ml dandelion
- 1 tbsp or 14.8 ml jasmine

If you want to use oils, combine the following:

- 4 drops rose oil
- 1 drop chamomile oil
- 2 drops rosemary oil
- 1 drop peppermint oil
- 4 drops lavender oil
- 4 drops jasmine oil
- 2 tbsps carrier oil

## WINTER WOODS:
## FULL MOON ESSENTIAL OIL BLEND

Prepare under a full moon and use to enhance winter meditations. This blend promotes comfort and assurance and strengthens your connection to the energy of winter and snow-laden branches. If using in a warm bath, this blend may be added directly into the bath. As the bathwater cools, the energy of this blend will amplify its effects.

- 4 drops pine needle oil
- 2 drops Atlas cedar oil
- 2 drops lavender oil
- 2 drops Virginian cedarwood oil
- 5 tbsps carrier oil (if using directly on skin) or 1 tbsp (if using in bath)

## WINTER WELLBEING:
## NEW MOON ESSENTIAL OIL BLEND

Prepare just before a new moon to empower rituals preformed during the dark half of the year, especially appropriate for the deep wintry months. This blend is used to calm the soul and promote a sense of assurance and well-being when working with the energy of a winter's new moon. If using in a warm bath, this blend may be added directly into the bath. As the bathwater cools, the energy of this blend will amplify its effects.

- 5 drops lavender
- 3 drops jasmine
- 2 drops peppermint
- 5 tbsps carrier oil (if using directly on skin) or 1 tbsp (if using in bath)

## FOREST FASCINATION:
## FULL MOON ESSENTIAL OIL BLEND

Prepare and use for a series of meditations conducted during and around the full moon of a summer month. The blend promotes a sense of support, security, and safety while encouraging you to journey to a forest in the summer. If using in a warm bath, this blend may be added directly into the bath. The energy of this blend is strongest when the bath is warmest and begins to fade as the water cools.

- 5 drops Virginian cedarwood oil
- 2 drops Indian sandalwood oil
- 2 drops patchouli oil
- 1 drop blood orange oil
- 5 tbsps carrier oil (if using directly on skin) or 1 tbsp (if using in bath)

## MYSTICAL WAYS AND ANCIENT DAYS:
## FULL MOON ESSENTIAL OIL BLEND

This blend encourages a connection to your mystical past. It can be used to enhance a meditation and is focused on growth. It can also be used to promote and strengthen a better working relationship with your magickal ancestors. This blend works best when used in the late summer to early autumn months. Follow safety guidelines to dilute with a carrier oil when using as an anointing oil for the third eye. If using in a warm bath, this blend may be added directly into the bath. The energy of this blend is strongest when the bath is warmest and begins to fade as the water cools.

- 1 drop vetiver
- 4 drops sandalwood
- 2 drops orange blossom
- 2 drops English rose
- 1 drop labdanum
- 5 tbsps carrier oil (if using directly on skin) or 1 tbsp (if using in bath)

## SPRINGTIME LIFT:
## NEW MOON ESSENTIAL OIL BLEND

Use this blend to promote a sense of action and continuity as part of a new moon ritual performed in the early days of spring. Gently wake up your spirit as you prepare to leave hibernation and let your mind begin the process of planning for the future. This blend is naturally uplifting and has the magickal property of providing a sense of guidance to your working. If using in a warm bath, this blend may be added directly into the bath. The energy of this blend is strongest when a warm bath begins to cool and a slight chill in the water is noticed. Add additional warm water to energize this blend, and then let its energy naturally fade.

Combine equal parts:

- Lemon
- Lavender

- Rosemary

- Carrier oil at a 2% dilution rate for use on skin or 1–2 tbsps for bath

## NEW INSIGHTS IN WINTER:
## NEW MOON LOOSE INCENSE BLEND

Prepare just before a new moon to empower rituals preformed during the dark half of the year, especially appropriate for the deep wintry months. This blend is used to clear negativity from a sacred working space, enliven the mind, invigorate the spirit, and promote a calm and protective atmosphere appropriate for guided meditations focused on exploring your inner landscape. Always burn incense in a well-ventilated space.

Combine equal parts:

- Frankincense resin, ground to a powder

- Eucalyptus leaves, ground to a powder

- Rosemary, ground to a powder

- Lavender flowers

- 9 drops rose oil

## GRAIL DRAGON INCENSE RECIPE

This is a variation of my Grail Incense recipe from *Arthurian Magic*.[20] While the Grail Dragon is not necessarily synonymous with the Holy Grail from the Arthuriana, it is a dragon whose energy can be tapped for healing and comfort.

Prepare under a full moon and use to enhance physical or spiritual healing and spiritual growth. This blend promotes comfort, assurance, and strengthens one's connection to the energy of the healing power of the Grail.

- Red rose petals, dried

- White oak bark, shaved and dried

---

20. John Matthews and Caitlín Matthews, *Arthurian Magic: A Practical Guide to the Wisdom of Camelot*, with Virginia Chandler (Woodbury, MN: Llewellyn Publications, 2017), 527.

- Dragon's blood resin
- Rosemary
- Frankincense resin
- Powdered coral

Use equal parts of the rose petals and white oak bark and grind together. Add dragon's blood until the mixture becomes a deep red color. Add just enough frankincense resin to smell the aroma within the mixture. Add a bit of powdered coral and grind again.

## YULETIDE DRAGON INCENSE RECIPE

Prepare under a full moon and use to enhance the Yuletide season. This blend promotes joy, warmth, and well-being, and strengthens one's connection to the energy of the winter dragons. This recipe is designed to help celebrate the Yuletide season and specifically honor the Yuletide dragon energy.

- White oak bark, shaved and dried
- Rosemary
- Frankincense resin
- Myrrh resin
- Cedar tips

Grind equal parts of the white oak bark and rosemary together. Add the frankincense resin in small measure (just enough that you can smell it), and then do the same for the myrrh resin. Add a dash of cedar tips and grind again.

## COMPANION DRAGON INCENSE RECIPE

Prepare under a full moon and use to aid in seeking a dragon companion or to honor a dragon companion. This blend sends a message of respect, purpose, and alliance. This recipe is designed to honor, seek, and connect with the energy of a companion dragon.

- Oak chips
- Rosemary
- Dragon's blood resin
- Oakmoss resin

Combine equal parts of all ingredients except the oakmoss resin. Grind until mixture is fine. Add a wee dash of oakmoss resin. Grind again.

## ELDER DRAGON INCENSE RECIPE

This recipe is designed to honor, seek, and connect with the energy of an elder dragon. Prepare under a full moon and use to honor the energy of the elder dragons. This blend sends a message of respect and pride.

- Frankincense resin
- Myrrh resin
- Rosemary
- Dragon's blood resin

Combine equal parts of all ingredients. Grind until mixture is fine.

## CONSECRATION OIL RECIPE

This oil recipe can be used to consecrate yourself, your magickal tools, and your sacred space.

- 2 tbsp or 30 ml frankincense oil
- 7 drops dragon's blood oil
- 5 drops patchouli oil
- 3 drops sandalwood oil
- 1 drop water
- Carrier oil at a 2% dilution rate for use on skin
- 3 breaths (yours) upon the mixed oils (adds your energy to the mixture)

Combine oils first, and then use a 2% dilution rate for the carrier oil based on how many drops of the mix you'll be using.

## DRAGONSONG INCENSE RECIPE

This oil recipe is designed to celebrate music and song with the energy of the dragons. Prepare under a full moon and use to aid in celebrating with the dragons. This blend sends a message of fun, rhythm, and joy.

- Dragon's blood resin
- Rosemary, dried
- Thyme, dried
- Amber resin

Use equal parts of the dragon's blood and amber resin and combine using pestle and mortar (or your own preferred grinding method). Add the thyme and rosemary in equal measure and grind again.

# APPENDIX B

## DRAGON SPELLS

Lists of dragon spells can be found in the ancient writings of Seneca, Apollonius Rhodius, Valerius Flaccus, and more. In these writings, dragon magick is described in surprising detail. Each ancient dragon spell presented in this appendix is broken down by the original source, spellcaster, magickal tools, myth or tale, and a modern interpretation.

For our purposes, a *charm* is defined here as an inanimate object that is infused with energy that is specific to a purpose. Sleep charms, love charms, and protection charms are examples. A *chant* is an oral component of a spell that is usually spoken in cadence or sung using language; chants can also be vocalizations of nonlanguage sound. An *incantation* is a composition of words that follows a certain rhythm or rhyme pattern. The intent of the spell is included in the words.

### PETITION FOR DRAGON AID

**Source:** Seneca, *Medea* (Roman epic, first century CE)

**Spellcaster:** Medea

**Magickal tool:** Voice

**Myth or Tale:** *Jason and the Argonauts*

## Incantation

*In answer to my incantations*
*Let Python come ...*
*Let Hydra return ...*
*Thou, too, ever-watchful dragon,*
*quitting the Colchians,*
*come thou to my aid,*
*thou who through my incantations*
*wast first lulled to slumber.*[21]

## Modern Interpretation

When Medea casts this spell and calls for the dragons to come to her, she is in danger and has a desperate need to make a hasty exit. She calls upon the great Greek dragons—Python, Hydra, and even the Dragon of Colchis—to come to her aid. Interestingly, it is not those dragons who come to her aid; instead, Medea's grandfather, the sun god, Helios, sends her a chariot that is drawn by a pair of Prime Mover dragons. Medea easily escapes without injury.

For a modern dragon practitioner, Medea's incantation can be modified to call for the aid of dragons who are known to the seeker and who are most likely to respond to the petition for help:

*In answer to my call,*
*I call upon [dragon ally].*
*I call upon [dragon ally].*
*I call upon [dragon ally].*
*Come to my aid*
*In this time of great need.*

---

21. Seneca, "Medea," in *Seneca's Tragedies*, vol. 1, trans. Frank Justus Miller (London: William Heinemann; New York: G. P. Putnam's Sons, 1917), 289.

# SLEEP CHARM

There are two separate sources that provide information about Medea putting the dragon of Colchis to sleep.

**Source 1:** Valerius Flaccus, *Argonautica* (Roman epic, third century BCE)

**Spellcaster:** Medea

**Magickal tool:** Voice, possibly singing

**Myth or Tale:** *Jason and the Argonauts*

## Incantation

An invocation to Hypnos, Greek god of sleep

> *All-powerful Sleep, from all the quarters of the world do I the maid of Colchis summon thee and bid thee descend upon the snake alone; oft with thy horn have I subdued waves and clouds and lightning brands and all that gleams in heaven; but now, now come to my aid with mightier influence, most like thy brother Death.*[22]

**Source 2:** Apollonius Rhodius, *The Argonautica* (Greek epic, third century BCE)

**Spellcaster:** Medea

**Magickal tools:** Voice

**Myth or Tale:** *Jason and the Argonauts*

**Spell components:** Juniper dipped in sleeping potion

## Incantation

> *But she with a newly cut spray of juniper, dipping and drawing untempered charms from her mystic brew, sprinkled his eyes, while she chanted her song; and all around the potent scent of the charm cast sleep; and on the very spot he let his jaw sink down; and far behind through the wood with its many trees were those countless coils stretched out. Hereupon Jason snatched the*

---

22. Valerius Flaccus, *Argonautica*, book 8, trans. J. H. Mozley, Theoi, accessed June 20, 2023, https://www.theoi.com/Text/ValeriusFlaccus1.html.

*golden fleece from the oak, at the maiden's bidding; and she, standing firm,*
*smeared with the charm the monster's dead, till Jason himself bade her turn*
*back towards their ship, and she left the grove of Areas, dusky with shade.*[23]

## Modern Interpretation

When Medea casts this spell, she is aiding her lover, Jason, in stealing the
Golden Fleece. She does not wish to harm the guardian dragon, and so she
uses her magick to lull him to sleep. The dragon does fall into a gentle slumber, and as Medea will call upon him at a later time, it can be assumed that he
is unharmed from the spell.

Medea's spell can be modified and used as a gentle persuasion for good
rest. Combine the smoky aroma of juniper with rosewood or patchouli, both
in equal parts, and burn this as an incense. Apply juniper oil mixed with carrier oil to the forehead with an incantation to the dream dragon, and a deep,
restful sleep is likely to occur.

**Spell components:** Juniper oil (and carrier oil) or juniper burned with rosewood or patchouli

*All-powerful Dream Dragon,*
*From all the quarters of the world*
*Do I, [your name], call you.*
*I invite you to descend upon [who needs the rest].*
*Your song of sleep*
*Has subdued waves and clouds and lightning,*
*And all that gleams in heaven.*
*Now come to my aid with your song of sleep.*

## PETITION FOR A GUARDIAN DRAGON

**Source:** Valerius Flaccus, *Argonautica* (Roman epic, third century BCE)

**Spellcaster:** King Aeetes of Colchis

**Magickal tool:** Voice

**Myth or Tale:** *Jason and the Argonauts*

---

23. Apollonius Rhodius, *The Argonautica*, trans. R. C. Seaton (London: William Heinemann,
1921), 305.

## Incantation

> *Gradivus,*
> *in whose sacred oak the fleece doth glitter,*
> *keep watch;*
> *present to aid*
> *let thy arms clash and trumpets sound in thy grove*
> *and thy voice ring through the darkness.*[24]

This text appears within a larger scene where King Aeetes prays to Ares (Gradivus):

> *"Thou too, Gradivus, in whose sacred oak the fleece doth glitter, keep watch; present to aid let thy arms clash and trumpets sound in thy grove and thy voice ring through the darkness." Scarce had he spoken, when a serpent gliding from the Caucasus mountains, not without the will of the god, entwined all the grove with its circling coils and looked toward the Grecian land. Therefore is he watchful to foil all threats and the dangers foretold by Phrixus.*[25]

## Modern Interpretation

King Aeetes petitions the god Ares to send him a guardian for Zeus's Golden Fleece. Likewise, when we have something precious that we wish to come to no harm, we can also request a guardian dragon. A more modern call for this energy request might be:

> *Oh, ancient and mighty dragons,*
> *Whose protection is a mighty gift,*
> *I, [your name],*
> *Ask that you keep watch over [what or who needs protection].*
> *I ask that your mighty arms clash like thunder when danger approaches,*
> *That your trumpets sound fair warning,*
> *And that your voice rings through the*
> *Darkness of any dangers to [what or who needs protection].*

---

24. Flaccus, *Argonautica*, book 5.

25. Flaccus, *Argonautica*, book 5.

## PETITION FOR WATER AND RAIN

**Source:** Ancient Chinese dragon lore

**Spellcaster:** Common folk, farmers

**Magickal tools:** Voice and body movement

The dragons of Chinese lore are powerful yet benevolent creatures. Many of these dragons are elemental dragons that are in a symbiotic relationship with the element of water. In ancient China, the people viewed dragons as symbols of wealth and luck, and "ancient farmers thought dragons brought much-needed rains and water to aid their crops."[26]

To thank the dragons and encourage them to be generous with the rains, the villagers would perform a processional dance, and "small dragons were made of pottery or banners were carried with a depiction of a dragon and written prayers asking for rain. Attendants would follow the procession carrying buckets of water and, using willow branches, they would splash onlookers and cry 'Here comes the rain!'"[27]

### Modern Interpretation

When the rain has been scarce and the land is in great need of water, go outdoors and take a drum or other musical instrument. Begin a slow, steady beat and visualize the rain clouds forming in the sky overhead. Repeat these words three times:

*Bring us the rain, oh Great Dragon!*

Continue the chant as you visualize the sky dragons coming together to form rain clouds. Imagine the rain falling from the sky and kissing the parched earth below. Perform this spell daily with the movement, declaration, and visualization until the rains begin.

---

26. Cartwright, "The Dragon in Ancient China."
27. Cartwright, "The Dragon in Ancient China."

# KEEPING THE BALANCE

Source: *The Book of Overthrowing Apep*

Spellcaster: Egyptian priests

Magickal tool: Voice

## Incantation

*Spitting Upon Apep*
*Defiling Apep with the Left Foot*
*Taking a Lance to Smite Apep*
*Fettering Apep*
*Taking a Knife to Smite Apep*
*Putting Fire Upon Apep*[28]

## Modern Interpretation

The giant serpent called Apep is a chaos dragon engaged in the cyclic battle for power with the solar deity, Ra, and Ra's dragon companion, Mehen. This battle between Apep and Ra keeps the world in balance. The individual spells in the incantation above would be used by priests to help Ra and Mehen defeat Apep over and over again.

Hence, our modern interpretation is a spell keeping chaos in check. We can never banish chaos—it is an integral element of the cosmos. But we can focus our energy and participate in holding the chaos at bay with the following chant:

*I say this to you, Chaos Dragon,*
*I place here my left foot.*
*[Place left foot forward and stomp your foot once.]*
*I smite the chaos dragon with my hands,*
*[Clap your hands together once.]*
*Slowing chaos.*
*I place here my right foot.*

28. E. A. Wallis Budge, *The Gods of the Egyptians: Or Studies in Egyptian Mythology*, vol. 1, Studies in Egyptian Mythology in Two Volumes (New York: Dover Publications, 1969), 325.

*[Place right foot forward and stomp your foot once.]*
*It is done.*

## PROTECTION SPELL

There are two separate sources that provide information about the Helm of Awe.

**Source 1:** Icelandic folktale, "There Is a Simple Helm of Awe Working"

**Spellcaster:** Fafnir, Guardian Dragon

**Magickal tool:** Voice

**Myth or Tale:** Sigurd and Fafnir

### Incantation

*Make a helm of awe in lead, press the lead sign between the eyebrows, and speak the formula:*

Ægishjálm er ég ber
milli brúna mér!

I bear the helm of awe
between my brows!

*Thus a man could meet his enemies and be sure of victory.*[29]

**Source 2:** *The Poetic Edda,* "The Lay of Fafnir"

**Spellcaster:** Fafnir, Guardian Dragon

**Magickal tool:** Voice

**Myth or Tale:** Sigurd and Fafnir

---

29. Jón Árnason, *Icelandic Folk and Fairy Tales,* selected and trans. May Hallmundsson and Hallberg Hallmundsson (Reykjavik, Iceland: Iceland Review, 1987), quoted in Stephen Flowers, *The Galdrabók: An Icelandic Grimoire* (York Beach, ME: Samuel Weiser, Inc., 1989), 100.

## Incantation

*The Helm of Terror I held over men*
*as I lay guarding the gold;*
*I found no one I had to fear,*
*few were worth a fight.*[30]

## Modern Interpretation

Although a helm usually conjures the image of a piece of armor to be worn on the head, it is most likely that Fafnir and other users of this power are referring to a stave or rune spell.

Rune magick is a powerful practice. If you are called to use the runes as part of your magickal practice, study them and their lore with passion. Learn them well. Here, runes and dragon energy are joined together for an immensely powerful energy working.

The Helm of Awe is an impressive and amazing arrangement of runes. The stave has eight arms that originate from a center and move outward in a defensive posture. Anything that manages to get past the outer ring will most certainly be trapped and crushed by the inner symbols.

*The Helm of Awe rune stave*

30. Terry, "The Lay of Fafnir," 154.

The intimidation evoked by the Helm of Awe is precisely what Fafnir and others who have used it intended.

To invoke the protection of the Helm of Awe, trace the rune stave, beginning with the center ring, upon the brow of what or who needs the protection. Speak the words:

> *See the Helm of Awe,*
> *Here upon my brow.*
> *It holds me in the protection of the gods*
> *To protect me from enemies all.*

# RECOMMENDED READING LIST

In addition to the specific titles listed below, there are certain authors whose work I particularly recommend: All books by Caitlín Matthews and John Matthews, Dolores Ashcroft-Nowicki, Gareth Knight, Joseph Campbell, Kahlil Gibran, and Dion Fortune.

## Greco-Roman Myth and Lore

*Metamorphoses*, Ovid
*The Greek Myths*, Robert Graves
*Myths of Greece and Rome*, Thomas Bulfinch

## Celtic Myth and Lore

*The Mabinogion*, Lady Charlotte Guest, trans.
*Encyclopedia of Celtic Wisdom*, Caitlín Matthews and John Matthews

## Egyptian Myth and Lore

*The Egyptian Book of the Dead*, available in various translations
*Gods of Ancient Egypt*, Barbara Watterson

## General Magick

*The Ritual Magic Workbook*, Dolores Ashcroft-Nowicki
*Living Magical Arts*, R. J. Stewart
*Advanced Magical Arts*, R. J. Stewart

## Ritual

*The Psychology of Ritual*, Murry Hope

## Runes

*Futhark*, Edred Thorsson
*Runelore*, Edred Thorsson
*The Runic Workbook*, Tony Willis

## Sound and Sonics

*The Spiritual Dimensions of Music*, R. J. Stewart
*Music and the Elemental Psyche*, R. J. Stewart
*Singing the Soul Back Home*, Caitlín Matthews

# BIBLIOGRAPHY

Aelian. *On the Characteristics of Animals.* Vol. 3, books 12–17. Translated by A. F. Scholfield. London: William Heinemann, Ltd., 1959.

*The Anglo-Saxon Chronicle: Part 2: AD 750–919.* The Medieval & Classical Literature Library. Accessed March 21, 2023. http://mcllibrary.org /Anglo/part2.html.

Árnason, Jón. *Icelandic Folk and Fairy Tales.* Selected and translated by May Hallmundsson and Hallberg Hallmundsson. Reykjavik, Iceland: Iceland Review, 1987.

Budge, E. A. Wallis. *The Gods of the Egyptians: Or Studies in Egyptian Mythology.* Vol. 1. Studies in Egyptian Mythology in Two Volumes. New York: Dover Publications, 1969.

Cartwright, Mark. "The Dragon in Ancient China." World History Encyclopedia. September 29, 2017. https://www.worldhistory.org/article/1125 /the-dragon-in-ancient-china/.

Flaccus, Valerius. *Argonautica.* Books 5 and 8. Translated by J. H. Mozley. Theoi. Accessed June 20, 2023. https://www.theoi.com/Text/Valerius Flaccus1.html.

Flowers, Stephen. *The Galdrabók: An Icelandic Grimoire*. York Beach, ME: Samuel Weiser, Inc., 1989.

Gardner, Gerald. *The Gardnerian Book of Shadows*. 1957. Sacred Texts. https://www.sacred-texts.com/pag/gbos/gbos36.htm.

Herodotus. *The Histories of Herodotus*. Translated by Henry Cary. New York: D. Appleton and Company, 1904.

Ingram, Simon. "What Makes Glastonbury so Mystical." National Geographic. Updated 14 May 2021. https://www.nationalgeographic.co.uk/history-and-civilisation/2019/06/what-makes-glastonbury-so-mystical.

Long, Leon. "Everything You Want to Know about Dragon Worship in China." China Educational Tours. N.d. https://www.chinaeducationaltours.com/guide/dragon-in-china.htm.

Mabie, Hamilton Wright. *Heroes Every Child Should Know*. Garden City, NY: Doubleday, Page & Company, 1907.

Martinif. "Throwing Virgins into the Sea and Other Ways to Appease the Gods: The Ancient Reasons Behind Virgin Sacrifice." Ancient Origins. Updated October 9, 2017. https://www.ancient-origins.net/history/throwing-virgins-sea-and-other-ways-appease-gods-ancient-reasons-behind-virgin-sacrifice-021653.

Matthews, John, and Caitlín Matthews. *Arthurian Magic: A Practical Guide to the Wisdom of Camelot*. With Virginia Chandler. Woodbury, MN: Llewellyn Publications, 2017.

Ovid. *Metamorphoses*. New York: Penguin Classics, 2004.

Pearson, Joanne. *A Popular Dictionary of Paganism*. New York: RoutledgeCurzon, 2002.

Polo, Marco. *The Travels of Marco Polo*. Translated by William Marsden. Edited by Manuel Komroff. New York: Modern Library, 2001.

Radford, Benjamin. "The Lore and Lure of Ley Lines." Live Science. Future US, Inc. November 19, 2013. https://www.livescience.com/41349-ley-lines.html.

Rhodius, Apollonius. *The Argonautica*. Translated by R. C. Seaton. London: William Heinemann, 1921.

Seneca, "Medea," in *Seneca's Tragedies*. Vol. 1. Translated by Frank Justus Miller. London: William Heinemann; New York: G. P. Putnam's Sons, 1917.

"Stars." NASA. Accessed April 5, 2023. https://science.nasa.gov/astrophysics/focus-areas/how-do-stars-form-and-evolve.

Terry, Patricia, trans. "The Lay of Fafnir." In *Poems of the Elder Edda*. Philadelphia: University of Pennsylvania Press, 1990.

Tolkien, J. R. R. *The Legend of Sigurd and Gudrún*. Edited by Christopher Tolkien. New York: Houghton Mifflin Harcourt, 2009.

"What Is Electromagnetic Energy?" Reference. Ask Media Group, LLC. March 29, 2020. https://www.reference.com/science-technology/electromagnetic-energy-118c0f3e43f35ef.

Zimmermann, Kim Ann. "Draco Constellation: Facts About the Dragon." Space. Future US Inc. July 20, 2017. https://www.space.com/16755-draco-constellation.html.

## TO WRITE TO THE AUTHOR

If you wish to contact the author or would like more information about this book, please write to the author in care of Llewellyn Worldwide Ltd. and we will forward your request. Both the author and publisher appreciate hearing from you and learning of your enjoyment of this book and how it has helped you. Llewellyn Worldwide Ltd. cannot guarantee that every letter written to the author can be answered, but all will be forwarded. Please write to:

Virginia Chandler
℅ Llewellyn Worldwide
2143 Wooddale Drive
Woodbury, MN 55125-2989

Please enclose a self-addressed stamped envelope for reply,
or $1.00 to cover costs. If outside the U.S.A., enclose
an international postal reply coupon.

Many of Llewellyn's authors have websites with additional
information and resources. For more information,
please visit our website at http://www.llewellyn.com.